GIRLS GONE OLD

GIRLS GONE OLD

essays by fiona helmsley

We Heard You Like Books • Los Angeles, California

PUBLISHED BY WE HEARD YOU LIKE BOOKS
A Division of U2603 LLC
5419 Hollywood Blvd, Ste C-231 Los Angeles CA 90027

http://weheardyoulikebooks.com/

Joshua Mast
Publisher

Brandon Creighton
Co-Publisher

Distributed by SCB Distributors

ISBN: 978-0-9964218-5-0
Copyright © 2017 by Fiona Helmsley

Some of the essays in this book first appeared online, in different versions.
2002: An Internet Odyssey at Hobart; *Secondary Sins* at Human Parts on
Medium; *Girls Gone Old*, and *Playing the Donald Trump Game* at
The Weeklings; *Flash Non-Fictions* at the Fanzine; *My Icon Hates Me* at Vol.1
Brooklyn; *Killing Me Softly: On Elliot Rodger, and the Power of No* at the
Feminist Wire; and *Ghoul Girl Grows Up* at Cherrybleeds (way back in 2008).

Typeset by Iphgenia Baal

Cover Image © 1970 The Associated Press
Used with Permission

August 2017

10 9 8 7 6 5 4 3 2 1

GIRLS GONE OLD

For Lou and Rachel and the kids at P.S. 192

I have no way to evaluate these things, no context in which to put them, it is true. But maybe the idea of fucking the lollipop girl or torturing the bound woman is like Danny Conrad's kiss. I fantasized about it all summer, but when it happened—a sticky lamprey-like attack—I didn't want it. Until later, when in fantasy, I wanted it again.

-Judith Levine

So, instead of the Internet I will make a little shop
In an art gallery and tell no one
In my dirty leopard coat it will be 1992 forever

Burned out hamburger sign in the foreseeable distance
Why am I tired of the Internet
Well where is my pussy, my old old pussy
No, my pussy belongs in the hallowed books of yore

-Dorothea Lasky

there was a girl whose boyfriend backhanded her in the face as a prelude to sex. she didn't know how she felt about it, it wasn't like it really hurt. of course, it did hurt, it was a real backhand, right to her cheekbone, but the pain was more a sting that dissipated quickly, and she was more shocked that he had done it than anything else. he had read some things that she'd written, and interpreted them quite literally. of course, that means nothing, you just don't backhand someone in the face as a prelude to sex because you think they want it, something like that has to live inside of you first.

-Facebook Cares About Your Memories

MY ICON HATES ME

My icon hates me. I suppose I shouldn't be surprised. Men we've had in common told me that one day this might be the case. Not because of any inherent belief they had in me, or my talents, but because of what they'd seen from her before. They described her disdain for other women like recognition, commendation. I'd gotten involved with most of them because of her. I'd taken the words I'd heard in 7th grade health class dead-seriously: *you have sex with all the partners your partners had sex with*. I had sex with them to have sex with her. Also, they were cute. She always had sex with the cutest guys.

By what they'd said, I could chart my *ascension* in our interactions. The first time I'd met her was at one of her shows, in the mid-1990s. I was wearing a ripped up, ragged dress, like the ripped up, ragged dresses she used to wear in the late 1970s. I had her haircut from then, too: a big, messy, mullet, blue-black, it's mulletness obscured by its messiness. There weren't many people at the show. My icon never had a huge following. We didn't want to share her much, anyway.

A friend and I were outside when she breezed past. "(NAME REDACTED)!" I said. It just came out. I'm a tactful person, though I did learn a degree of boldness approaching her ex-flames. "Hey," she said. Her pale skin glowed. Her lips were red, red, red, like blood on snow. She was in her late 30s then, my friend and I, barely legal, costumed versions of her. "I have to go," she said, gesturing towards the entrance. "These two," she said to the man collecting money nearby, "They don't pay." She smelled like highly realized patchouli. Patchouli that had turned its back on non-violence.

Inside, my friend and I stood near the side of the stage. I noticed my friend Paul by the bar, and waved. At the time, female-led bands would ask that the women at their shows move to the front, to form a shield against the men in the crowd dancing wildly and copping feels. The men at my icon's show were way too cool for such shenanigans, but between songs, she asked that my friend and I move from our spot to the front of the stage. Looking back, I think she wanted us to stand there so she could sing *down* on us.

When the show ended, my icon left. I looked around for Paul, but he was also gone. They'd left together.

Paul was my age, and like me, he'd sought out the people who had made up her circle at different times. Her associates were a who's who of grimy art world cool. Besides music, she'd starred in 8MM films. She'd written books, with blood-red book marks attached. While I had sex with the men she'd collaborated with, Paul brown-nosed them, and wrote about them for xeroxed periodicals.

He moved in with her. They co-wrote a book about subway station sexual encounters, made a film about a stringy-haired co-ed killer. They began working on an anthology, and Paul asked me to contribute a story. I did and he said my icon loved what I wrote.

Liar!

Her writing was always about the uglier aspects of life. Bad things happened. People reacted worse. It was presented as thinly veiled fiction: for me, confirmation (by the context clues) as to the identities of all the cute guys she'd had sex with. She presented herself as the one who was always in control, unable to be exploited, because she was the ultimate exploiter. ABANDON ALL HOPE YE WHO ENTER was the title of one of her books. It was general knowledge that its title referred to her vagina.

I'd been writing since I was a child, and had first discovered my icon via a book called PISSED BITCHES. Her writing was explicit. Blunt. I would later incorporate these stylistic qualities into my own writing, especially a willingness to go into *minute* detail about my sex life.

It didn't work out with her and Paul. Despite their break-up, they remained friendly. Paul contacted me about the anthology's release, and invited me to the book party. My icon would be there. He'd make a formal introduction.

Coincidentally, I'd always had a slight interest in Paul, free of the aphrodisiac-like stigmata he now presented as her former conquest. The party would be the first time I'd seen him since their split. It had been almost five years.

Paul was drunk, but looked the same. My icon was heavier. She looked voluptuous; her basket of breasts overflowed. The crowd was mostly her male friends from her various projects: a few I knew intimately, others I hoped to become more familiar with in the future. I mingled, but stuck mostly by Paul. My icon passed us as we were talking, and Paul said:

"(NAME REDACTED), this is (NAME REDACTED). She wrote the (NAME REDACTED) story in the book. I told you she considers you to be a big influence."

My icon's body stiffened. It was as if a small woodland creature had burrowed its way into her asshole. She made Richard Gere face, a face I've never actually seen, but imagine as being like the one the actor made when the rodent entered his rectum. She turned from Paul to me. It was at that moment, I believe, she decided I was a disease: maybe tuberculosis, at the time of the Bronte's, maybe AIDS, circa 1985.

"What story?" she spat.

I wasn't sure if she was asking me the name of the story I'd written, or a story of her's that had influenced me. Either way, it felt like a test. Trying to cover both interpretations of the question, I stammered, "(NAME REDACTED), and I love (NAME REDACTED)." I felt like an unprepared pageant contestant.

She pulled Paul by the arm out of my earshot. I tried not to look over at them, and stared at the back of Michael Musto's head.

Paul returned. "Sorry," he said. "She's just stressed, because of Dordie Coment."

Dordie Coment was an underground actress and musician who had just found mainstream success with her band, THE GAPING

WOUNDS. Dordie's icon had been my icon, and she had spoken about our icon's influence in interviews.

"Oh (NAME REDACTED) paved the way. She was so fucking angry, and I was angry, too. PISSED BITCHES was like a call to marching orders. I mean a call to arms. I mean, marching orders. ABANDON HOPE ALL YE WHO ENTER? Fuck. After I read that, I embraced my inner see-you-next-Tuesday, and ran with her. Soon after, I formed THE GAPING WOUNDS."

I suppose praise from Dordie was open to interpretation depending on how you felt about Dordie. I liked Dordie, and enjoyed seeing her on TV. Our icon didn't, and let it be known, when she was asked her opinion about Dordie for a magazine article about her.

"Don't fucking blame me," my icon said. "I may have provided the egg, but I didn't baste her."

When Dordie had read what our icon had said about her by the writer doing the article, she lowered the boom on her praise *significantly*. "Well, please let (NAME REDACTED) know, if there is anything she needs, any tax-deductible thing, she can always contact my accountant, but he's Jewish, so she should be mindful of the Sabbath."

My icon had more to say after hearing Dordie's cheeky retort, but her response was relegated to a xeroxed periodical, done by Paul.

"Actually, I never said anything about that woman," my icon said. "How could I? I have no fucking idea who she is."

"Does she know Dordie?" I asked Paul.

"I mean, yeah, but it's not like they're friends or anything."

"Then why start that?" I asked. "Why say, 'I didn't baste her'?"

"I don't know. She can be weird with women sometimes. Dordie should take it as a compliment."

"I've heard that," I said. "Did she really tell you she liked my story, Paul?"

"I don't remember," he said. "It took so long for the book to come out. She really didn't have that much to do with it, anyway. Can I have a sip of your beer?"

As it turned out, Paul was the last sex partner my icon and I had in common.

❧

Years went by. The Spice Girls arrived. My icon became more robust. She still performed and wrote, but her name wasn't mentioned that much as an influence on cross-over culture. This surprised me, as I saw one-off versions of things she'd done first in the 1970s and 80s all the time. I knew there were others like Dordie, Paul, and myself, who had considered her to be a formative influence. Had those people just not done enough with their lives to warrant speaking about who had influenced them? Had my icon been the icon of choice for a generation of do-nothings?

Was she an... *anti-icon*?

Maybe she wasn't an anti-icon so much as her fans remained largely digitally illiterate, cut off from sharing their feelings about how inspirational she'd been. I wondered if the answer to her invisibility laid, to an extent, with the internet. The generation who had most actively felt her influence had also been the last to come of age without it. If we wanted to use this new communication tool, we had to learn how to ourselves. Web-surfing wasn't a hard thing to master, but people are often resistant to new technology. Whatever the reason, at the dawn of the new millennium, my icon still seemed relegated to the world of xeroxed periodicals.

I kept writing, and in the mid-2000s, I was asked to contribute an essay about the American Female Experience for a book by a European press. I wrote about my brief foray into teen prostitution — a foray no doubt inspired in some small part by my icon's role as a teen prostitute named Bambi in a series of underground films. The story after mine in the book was written by my icon. It was about her voracious appetite for sex and food, more food than sex, she wrote, as she got older.

Soon after, she got a website.

❧

I took inspiration from my icon's story in the book, and decided to write an article about all the cute guys she'd had sex with. The inspiration was, I would compare each guy to a different kind of food. For example, (NAME REDACTED) was compared to steak, because he was into weightlifting. Paul, who had made a name for himself as a Pete Doherty-type hot mess was compared to barley, because he drank. But something happened as I was doing research for the article. I reread the books and stories by my icon that had been so important to me when I was younger and realized I no longer thought they were all that good. The writing seemed amateurish.

Stunted. The perspective in the stories read to me as almost...*macho*? I'd had this happen before with other artists I'd considered formative: I had to admit I'd outgrown whatever it was about their work that had resonated so much with me. But you invest time in making your icons your icons. It can be hard to let go. I wrote the article, and it was published online. The editor of the European press who had put out the book we'd both been in told me he'd sent my icon the article, and that she loved it. I told him about a new project I was working on, about artists and their favorite sweaters. I asked him if he thought she might contribute. He gave me her email address, and told me to contact her. The name she was using for her email address sounded like it should have belonged to a Hot Topic Goth.

I composed this message:

Hey (NAME REDACTED),

I don't know if you remember me, but I hope you do. Your writing, music, and life has influenced me so much. I'm doing this project called SWEATERS OF COOL PEOPLE. It's pictures of artist's sweaters, with a few lines they've written about a memory they associate with the sweater. I've gotten some really great people to contribute. I'd love it if you would.

If you don't remember me, we've had stories in a few of the same books throughout the years. I also wrote an article about your ex-partners and their various "food signs." Thank you for all the years of inspiration.

(NAME REDACTED)

❧

I still talked to the friend who had come to the show with me the first time I had met my icon, all those years ago. To give you an idea of the amount of time that had passed since then, we could both wear mom jeans. Could, but didn't. We stayed stylish.

I messaged her as the days passed without a response from my icon. My friend worked a lot, and often wouldn't get back to me right away. Sometimes, it seemed like I was having a conversation with myself.

Day 2
It's not so much that I even want her to contribute to the sweater project. I mean, I do, I do, but it's like I

want some kind of confirmation from her acknowledging my existence.

Day 3
Not that her not acknowledging my existence would mean that I didn't exist. Nor would her acknowledgement mean I had some greater validity.

Day 4
At one point does one stop being a fan and become a peer? Does one have to stop acting like a fan to be a peer? Can I be a fan and a peer??

Day 5
Dordie fucking Coment will message with me. She steals my Facebook statuses! Who does (NAME REDACTED) think she is??

Day 6
Lest you think I'm not being considerate of (NAME REDACTED)'s 'agency', let me remind you, have you reviewed her body of work recently? She abuses and exploits other women all the time. She's worse than Bret Easton Ellis. Remember that anti-drug commercial that was on TV around the time we were obsessed with her? With the kid who smokes pot, and the dad who finds it, and is all "Who taught you this?" and the kid is all, "I learned by watching you dad, I learned by watching you!" That's her and me. I learned by watching you (NAME REDACTED)! I learned by watching you!!!!

Day 8
Do you think maybe she's in Europe?

No, my friend responded later that night. *I just saw online that she's doing spoken word around here. I hate spoken word, and have a hard time staying up past ten, but do you wanna go?*

ᔥ

A book of my short stories had just come out on a small press, and I brought a copy with me to give to my icon. I had thanked her in the book's acknowledgements. Despite my change of opinion when it came to the quality of her writing, it was never just her writing that had appealed to me. Like I'd written in the email I'd sent her (which she'd yet to respond to), it was the whole package of her — well, except the recent addition of the spoken word — but I understood. We all had bills to pay. Whatever it was I felt I'd outgrown about her, she was still a formative person in my life.

It was a small club, fairly crowded for a weeknight. My friend and I were sitting at the bar when my icon came in with the two men who made up her musical accompaniment.

"She's hereeeeee," my friend said, in the voice from the little girl from *Poltergeist.* We both turned towards the door.

"(NAME REDACTED)!" a very young, handsome, arty-looking guy said, approaching her as she came in. They embraced, then he opened a door by the bar, that led to a backroom.

There were two bands performing before her, and waiting for her to emerge from the back, I began to get impatient. And bored. And a bit drunk. My friend got tired, then crabby.

"We're too old for this," I said as a generic noise band comprised of found metallic objects began it's ear-splitting cacophony.

"And she's older than we are!" my friend said. "How does she take it? That's probably why she's hiding out in the back. She looks good, don't you think?"

She did. In the quick glimpse that I'd gotten of her, she looked great. She was almost 60. Twenty minutes later, my icon still hadn't come out, but I noticed one of her music men ferrying drinks back and forth between the bar and the backroom.

"Maybe this wasn't such a good idea," my friend said. "I have to work early in the morning."

I decided that was my cue, and approached him.

"Hey," I said. "I don't want to be annoying, but do you think (NAME REDACTED) is going to come out before she performs?"

"I don't know," he said.

"My friend and I are feeling a bit out of our element, but we've been fans of (NAME REDACTED) for awhile, and would like to say hi."

"Uh, I can ask her," he said. "But she's kind of anti-social."

"Maybe that's it," I said starting to feel the alcohol I'd been drinking. "Maybe that's the answer to the big riddle. Something so simple. Maybe it's not that she hates other women specifically, maybe it's just that she's anti-social…"

"The big riddle?" the man said.

"Well, throughout the years, that's always been my experience with her. When I've met her, she's never been particularly nice. Not that she has to be. I wrote this article about the men she's had sex with, and now I'm trying to get her to do this other project about sweaters…"

"Oh the list that compared her partners to food?"

"Yes!" I said.

"Oh, yeah, yeah! She loved that!"

"I had sex with some of those dudes because of her!"

"You know, you're not the first person I've heard say that," he said. "But she can be kind of weird about meeting people."

"I've met her before. Here," I said, deciding to hedge my bets.

"Can you give her this?" I handed him the copy of my book.

"I don't want to risk not getting it to her. I thank her in it. I don't know if my friend is going to make it much longer here."

"Okay," he said. "Give me a minute. I'll try to get her to come out."

♋

"I don't think she's coming out," my friend said, at the ten minute mark. "I think there are strippers and blow back there, and I don't think her music guy is coming back, either."

"I do," I said. "I believe."

A few minutes later I felt a tap on my shoulder.

I knew it was her.

"Here," her music man said. "I tried. She asked me to ask you what you have against spoken word."

"Huh?" I said. "I never said that to you. Did you tell her I said that? No! No!"

"She signed the book," he said.

"Signed the book?" I said, taking the copy of my book back into my hands. "I wrote this book! I was giving it to her! Look," I said, pointing to my name on the cover. "That's me!"

"Well, she signed it," he said, "Usually she's resistant to doing even that."

I opened the cover. She'd crossed out my name on the title page, and in big red letters she'd written her own: (NAME REDACTED).

If there was a message in it, I got it. And maybe she was right.

One person's "influence" is another person's "rip off."

The cliché is *kill your idols*. But maybe, if she's really worth your veneration, your icon finds a way to rub you out first.

GIRLS GONE OLD

On a busy Friday morning, a patron at the library where I work came up to the counter at the circulation desk, to tell me, with a degree of excitement, that she thought I looked a lot like her favorite fiction writer, Luanne Rice. I thanked her, but really had no idea what she was saying with the comparison, as I'd never seen a picture of Luanne before. I was curious, so when it quieted down, I went out to the stacks and pulled out one of Luanne's books to look at her author photo.

I could *kind of* see the resemblance: the color and style of our hair; the glasses. Luanne looks a bit like the stereotyped library lady, minus the bun:

The comparison got me thinking though, what female writer would I like to *think* that I look like? The first writer that came into my head was Elizabeth Wurtzel, the way she looked on the cover of her book, *Bitch*.

It might seem like a dated choice, but I'm a child of the 90s, what can I say.

Recently, I was accused of being a bit "dated" myself.

ℰℐ

A few weeks ago I was talking to a male acquaintance named Bill. Bill is in his mid-20s, and in a band. Tall and gangly, he resembles a sort of young, big-haired Robert Zimmerman. He lives about an hour away from me, in a city that I had some connection to a few years back. As Bill and I were talking, I mentioned Ted, a musician who I had met at a show there, a few years before. I was outside smoking a cigarette, and Ted approached me, and asked for my phone number. It was a bold move, considering he wasn't drunk. I thought Ted was cute; he looked Parisian in his grey scarf, so I gave it to him. He called, and we went out. I liked Ted, but learned there was an almost fifteen year age difference between us — I was almost fifteen years older. I had other things going on at the time, namely, a former skinhead in Brooklyn, and decided not to pursue anything further. Ted would still text me from time to time, saying he was thinking about me, and wondering how I was. He didn't seem to hold any resentment. Later, he got married, and though we don't really keep in touch, I would have considered us friends.

Bill said he knew Ted.

Coincidentally, he thought he would probably see him that weekend.

᎑

Yesterday I was talking to a male friend who is also a writer. He's a big fan of David Foster Wallace, as a lot of smarty-pants men in my age group seem to be. Our conversation drifted over to our thoughts about getting older, then, for some reason, he told me what he thought the aging process might mean for me.

"You take care of yourself," he said. "Exercise. Eat well. I don't think you have much to worry about. In the pictures you've been posting on Facebook lately, I think you're starting to look a bit like Mary Karr."

I liked being compared to Mary much more than Luanne. Luanne writes books about beaches and sandcastles, while Mary writes books about drinking, and essays comparing poetry to prayer. Mary also describes herself as a Cafeteria Catholic, and I consider myself a Cafeteria Catholic. I try to take the plate of alms for the poor, but take a pass on the servings of misogyny and homophobia.

⁊

After the weekend, I saw Bill again. "I saw Ted," he said. "Why didn't you tell me you guys were related?"

"Related?" I said. "Ted and I aren't related. Why would you think that?"

"I mentioned to Ted that I knew you, and he said you were his aunt."

ↄ∕ↄ

Last year I had a book come out, which meant I had to decide on a cover image — a visual to introduce me to you, free of us meeting in person. A small author photo on the back of the book would not suffice. I put myself on the cover of a book I published myself a few years ago, but I hate that book. I decided to just put my legs on the cover this time:

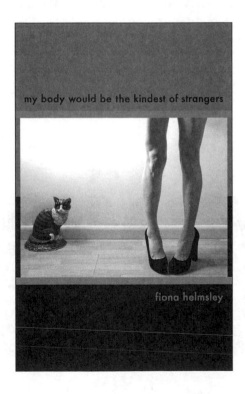

I don't trust people when it comes to what they read. I work with books, and know that most people don't take many risks. When it comes to books, most people either:

1. Read what their friends read
2. Heed the advice of disembodied strangers who sometimes have vested interest in what they are hyping so glowingly online and in newspapers/magazines
3. Equate the quality of the writing with the amount of money it's made for the author/publisher

The way I've sometimes dealt with this distrust in the past is by using my body — the thought being that if you as a potential reader found me physically attractive, you would be more likely to read my writing. It feels worse to admit to having done this than it ever felt to do it. Sometimes, it felt *good* to do it. Once, I considered making the book cover equivalent of this album cover:

I was a bit of an exhibitionist, but with an agenda. But the thing about this kind of exhibitionism, especially if you are a woman, is that it has a timestamp. You're trying to bait assholes. Eventually they won't want to look.

છ

What Ted had intimated to Bill with the word "aunt" was that I, the person he had boldly approached and pursued was *old*.

છ

When asked, famous women will often say that their motivation for doing *Playboy* and other fleshy pictorials is to mark that place, in body, and in time, when they felt they looked their best, so that in the future, when they no longer feel that way (or perhaps, more accurately, when they have *thoroughly internalized* that they should no longer feel that way), they can look back. They are making mementos of something they feel is worthy of documentation: *that time when I was hot*. I've done this. Since I got my first digital camera, I've taken thousands of photos of myself, naked and clothed, alone, and with a timer, with the help of boyfriends, and friends. I've made my own mementos, in preparation of something being lost.

What I never took into consideration was how this change in perception might make me feel.

For me, often, there is the in-principle, and the in-practice. There is what I believe, and how I have sometimes chosen to navigate my place in the world, a place where I felt both men and other women wouldn't always give me a fair shake. Sometimes my belief, and my practice didn't merge.

Sometimes they seemed to be diametrically opposed.

℘

It was like a contagion.

A female friend who is a college sophomore would see Bill and me talking. This female friend completely of her own volition, with zero push, nor approval, nor clearance from me, got the idea that Bill and I should get together. *You are both artistic, both well-read, both politically-minded*, she would later say. (Though, truth be told, Bill was much more *politically-minded* than I was: He had once popped a tire on his bicycle in a rainstorm, and instead of going to the Wal-Mart across the street to get a patch, *wheeled* his bike the two miles home. Bill did not support corporate America. To illustrate the point, he liked to share this story.) Completely of her own volition, with zero push, nor approval, nor clearance from me, she approached Bill with her idea.

I asked her afterward, *Why would you tell me you did this, something I never wanted you to do, in light of what he said? Why tell me that you'd even done it at all?*

Bill's response to my friend's idea about him and me was, *"She's weird and old."*

℘

I'm in my late 30s. I'm closer to 50 now than I am to 20. Though I believe that aging doesn't negate my value in any way, adjusting to the changing currents in how I am perceived is hard. Adjusting to the changing currents in how I am perceived — a way of valuing women that I think is vile, and repugnant, but have also used to suit my purposes — is hard. I chose to incorporate my physicality and sexuality into my identity as a writer. I liked the attention, but I also hoped in some ways that it would work as a leveler.

It was my choice. I was always very aware of what I was doing.

Since I chose to do this, I can say, upon reflection — the gains were pretty meager. I ended up having to deal with more fuckers than fans, and in the communications I had with a lot of the male readers of my writing, that undercurrent was always there, and never really seemed to morph into anything more substantial. Yes, they wanted to fuck me (false success), but it never really evolved, as far as I could tell, into some deeper appreciation of my work (real success). I've learned that women can use their physicality, but they will never be able to control what happens once they do.

Once I'd turned them on, it was hard to turn them off.

It was hard to get them to focus.

It was hard to get them to read.

When I was 25, I worked at a coffee shop with a 16 year-old girl named Rory. One afternoon, she was leafing through an old issue of *Rolling Stone* and came across an interview with Joe Francis, founder and creator of *Girls Gone Wild*.

"Uh-oh, Fiona!" she said. "Joe Francis says the cut off age to be a *Girls Gone Wild* girl is 25! That means no *Girls Gone Wild* for you!"

"Eww. Like I care what that slimy scumbag thinks," I said. Though this was 99% true, I did give a tiny little turd, because it was strange to think of myself as cut off from *anything*, regardless of the skeeve factor of the person making the decree.

ᴄʌ

Over the years, I used my body, and I have to say, though it was sometimes fun, it was mostly a trap. Maybe those times that I defaulted to it, I could have harnessed some other skill, a superior con, a better persuasion, to lead you to my mind. Maybe as a woman there is nothing you can do. Your physicality will always be part of the equation, and it's better to be the one in the driver's seat of the machinery. But I'm starting to wonder if I was always just the passenger. Maybe if I hadn't defaulted to it as often as I did, "old" wouldn't carry any sting. Maybe if I hadn't defaulted to it, "old" wouldn't make me feel like someone was trying to *take* something from me.

❦

There's another side to this, and it deserves to be mentioned.

When you use your physicality, you're playing with desire, and being desired is addictive. On the other side of physicality, of sexuality, as a potentially harnessable skill, there is physicality and sexuality as *thrill*. It's thrilling to be wanted. It can feel like power, and sometimes it is. Of course, there is good desire, and bad desire, unwelcome vs. welcome (you have to qualify everything today). But even harmless unwelcome desire can come with a kick. There is a look a man or a woman will give you when they meet you, it happens fast: it almost looks like an intimation of understanding, but you haven't said anything yet. It's based completely on the physical; it's nothing deeper than that. Maybe it's some kind of mating/reproductionary response, but when you've seen it enough times in dimly lit bars and sweaty clubs, or on the street, you can identify it. It is a superficial kind of want, but inherent to that want is an opportunity, and an option, and the recognition of that opportunity comes with a thrill.

Ted had given me this look the night he asked for my phone number.

Having known that look, I think I would miss it were it to disappear from my life.

But these are just my feelings now, two "olds" in. I also think of my grandmother, in the last year of her life. She was 95 and lived with a home health aide named Cleo who called her "Miss Rita." One morning while I was visiting, Cleo tried to cajole my grandmother from her chair in the living room into the bathroom to change out of her bed clothes. When my grandmother finally got up, she started taking her clothes off in front of a big picture window.

"Miss Rita!" Cleo said. "The whole neighborhood will see you naked!"

"Cleo," my grandmother said, standing there defiantly in her underwear, "They stopped wanting to look years ago. Please allow me to enjoy my freedom."

℘

Even though I was never interested in Bill, even though I hadn't wanted my friend to approach him and was embarrassed and angry that she did — what he'd said pissed me off, so I confronted him.

"'Weird' I will accept with bells on," I said. "For me, 'weird' is a point of pride. But I'm really surprised that you — you who claim to be so passionate about righting the wrongs of the world, you who went and lived in New York for two weeks during the Occupy demonstrations, you who wouldn't use a fucking bike patch from Wal-Mart — would default to the language of *The Man* and call me 'old.'"

What could he say?

Nothing.

So he denied it.

Said he'd never said it.

Flailed his arms. Jumped up and down. Asked me who told me that he said that, but he *knew*, because he said it. So did he really think I was "old"? Had Ted put the idea into his head and it stayed there, or had it grown there, organically, like the kale he so liked to eat?

Or was it something totally different, but just as insidious?

Had Bill called me "old" in the company of my younger female friend, as some kind of *posture*?

Later that week he asked me to come to one of his shows, on a Friday night.

"No, bro, I can't." I said. "Friday nights are bad for me. I play bridge and chug Metamucil with my best girls Dorothy and Sophia."

I wondered if he got "The Golden Girls" reference.

I stayed in that night. I reread *Bitch*. Then the next week at work I took out a book I'd been meaning to read for a while.

The Liar's Club, by Mary Karr.

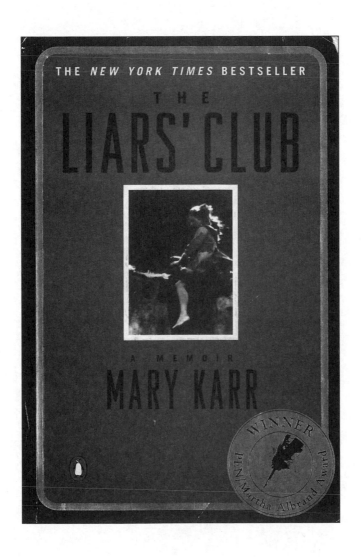

12 FLASH NON-FICTIONS

1. This afternoon, my son and I went to visit my mother at the school where she works. I went to school there as a kid, and I got into a lot of trouble, which was awkward, because the people I got into trouble with were all her co-workers and friends. As we were talking, a man came over to ask her a question. I recognized him as one of the deans from my senior year of high school, at the height of my badness. I was really, really bad. I pushed a teacher once, and hung the man in effigy in the hallway. Seeing him now, twenty years later, I had to say something, so I apologized. "Don't worry about it," he said. "I thought you were..." "Troubled?" I answered for him. "Yes," he said. "But I also thought you were funny. I remember this one time, I told you that you looked nice, do you remember what you said to me in response?" I shook my head. "Pervert!" he said. "You called me a pervert! I thought that was funny."

2. At age eleven I have a boyfriend. We are in the same homeroom class, and have daily journals that the teacher makes us keep, but does not read. Every morning, I come into school early with my mother, who works at the school, and while no one else is there, slip his journal out of his desk, and read it. He writes nice things about me that make me feel warm. Eventually, I go to his house, and we swim in his family's pool. I wear a purple bathing suit with a large grey tiger on the front. The next day at school, my male classmates won't stop laughing. They say that I am pregnant, that my boyfriend put his sperm in the pool. I turn to my boyfriend, expecting him to say something in our defense, but he puts his head down, and looks away.

3. My mom's big dream when I was a kid was to buy this medieval castle in Ireland and turn it into a bed and breakfast. The castle was on the market for a long time, and she kept the real estate listing for it in a dresser drawer in her bedroom. She hoped to get other people in our family to chip in, and they could all run it together, but no one was interested. I would see the picture of the castle whenever I went into her dresser to look for change, or a pair of socks. The dream in the drawer.

4. My dad grew up in Dublin in the 1930s. He came from a family with not a lot of money and the cliché of apples for Christmas applied. He had to drop out of school to work which made him insecure and on guard to prove his intellect. He hated *The Brits. The Brits.* "The Brits" was a slur I heard often growing up. I still hear it at family gatherings, especially when there is drinking. My father joined the IRA. He spent time in jail. I think he wished he spent more time there. When he was in his late twenties, he moved to New York. There is a black and white picture of my father in Dublin with his first wife right before they left: He is wearing a belted trench coat, and his hair is shiny with pomade. He stands on a street corner, his arms wrapped around his attractive young wife. *Promise.* They both look high on promise.

5. My father had a strange sense of humor. When we were bad, "The Turkey Man" was coming to get us. The Turkey Man was a winged, white meat monstrosity who flew through windows — a Thanksgiving Day Moloch whose favorite meal was cheeky kids. Another common threat of my father's was punishment by internment at "Rosemary Hall." Rosemary Hall, we were told, was a jail for children, run by sinister nuns, who enjoyed torturing young people in a sadistic frenzy. Rosemary Hall exists. It's a posh boarding school, a part of Choate. In actuality, what my father was threatening us with was a first class education — probably the thing he most wanted for himself.

6. I have a memory of being in my parent's room, standing between them on their bed, as they slept. In the memory, I am naked. I must be about seven or eight. There is a Mass card stuck to the mirror in front of me, the mirror, that in the memory, I am admiring my naked body in. I decide to memorize the prayer on the card; I will add it to the prayers that I say at night, before bed. I imagine that my mother will be very impressed when she hears me recite this new prayer at bedtime that I have learned of my own volition. The prayer on the card is the Serenity Prayer. Though there are things about this memory that I question, I never had to learn the Serenity Prayer once I began my decade in and out of drug treatment. I always knew it, always had it memorized. How did I learn it then?

7. Packing up the car with my mother and siblings: spending the night, or a few nights at my grandparent's, or my uncle's. The mad rush to get out the door before he returned from wherever he'd been drinking, it felt exciting, like an adventure. Pack — *fast!* Grab the dog — find the dog, *where's the dog?* Once, we forgot something: maybe it was an ID, or the name of a lawyer, or a homework assignment, and we had to go back. We passed him stumbling down the street. I watched him out the car window — we were racing him back to the house. *We were racing dad!* Running from my father meant we would be going to the park, so my mother and uncle could talk in hushed voices at the picnic table. It meant we were going to be eating at Wendy's. Running from my dad meant *fun.*

8. Something sort of quietly beautiful happened yesterday. My grandmother is in her 90s, and starting to get sick. Really, she is more depressed than anything, and at her age, it goes without saying, her body is tired. We were talking, her in her chair, her throne, and me close by on the couch. Her hearing is not good, and she won't wear her hearing aid. "How come you don't mention any men lately?" she asked me, not really seriously, more jovial. "Lately, I just don't care," I answered, truthfully. "But you know what, Gram? I've been thinking that I could really love a woman." I said it like I was kidding, though I wasn't. And my grandmother said, and I couald tell that she really meant it, "Well, there were plenty of times I felt that way, too."

9. I visit my grandmother a few times a week. Today, I went to see her with my mother and my son. "I have to tell you something," she said to me, a few minutes into our visit. "But I don't want you to get resentful." "What, Great Nana?" I said. I call her "Great Nana" when I'm with my son, because that's what he calls her. "On Sunday, your lipstick was too bright," she said. "Too bright?" I repeated. "You usually do it so well. Like right now, it looks nice. But on Sunday, your lipstick was much too bright." I looked over at my mom, who shrugged her shoulders. "Are you saying I looked like a hussy, Great Nana?" I asked. "I don't want you to get upset..." she said, twisting the end of the blanket she was sitting on. "And you let me leave your house like that, in my too bright lipstick, looking like a hussy?" "I didn't know what to say!" she said. On the ride home, I envisioned my grandmother seeing my too bright lips like beacons of light, hussy lighthouses calling out to lost crotches in the night.

10. When I still loved my son's father in an active and intoxicating way, I went through the dumpster behind our apartment. I climbed in while wearing shorts; the garbage was up to my kneecaps. I had a stick. I was looking for something. I wouldn't know what 'til I found it. Something that would make feel more in control, give my anger towards him a direction. Thankfully, I found what I needed quickly: a condom and a crushed beer can, the dented side of the can covered in thick ash. Thinking about it, all these years later, while the beer can was definitely his, the likelihood that the condom wasn't, is high.

11. When my son's father died, his sisters asked me to write his obituary. After I came up with a draft, I read it to his sister Rebecca over the phone. She liked it, but told me she thought I should include his "local" nickname. When he was younger, she explained, he'd worked in a restaurant, and was closely associated with his job there. She thought I should include the nickname in the obituary like this: his first name, quotes around the nickname, then his last name. "What's the nickname?" I asked. "Johnny Hamburger," she said. "Oh," I said. "He never told me that. Can I call you back?" I immediately got on the phone with his other sister, Michelle. "I don't want to fight with anyone," I said. "I want you all to be in our son's life forever, but I can't do it. I can't give John to eternity, even if it's just on paper, as 'Johnny Hamburger.' It makes him sound like a Happy Meal character, or a murdered mafioso. Maybe I'm superficial, but I can't." My mind had already gone to a million bad places. I imagined John's final send-off held up in court, as I battled his sisters over this small detail. I might have done it, too, I felt so strongly about it. "Thank God," Michelle said, "I said 'no' too, but then relented a bit, and said she should ask you."

12. We were talking about the essay I wrote about my son's father's death, and how, whenever he checked himself into treatment, he'd always dress to look his best. And we were talking about how, unless you come from money, by the time you're willing to check yourself in somewhere, there's usually not much wiggle room around it: you look as ruined as you feel. We talked nothing about why he always made the effort. And we talked about how I haven't been in treatment since 2004, but by that time I'd tried it close to 20 different times, and there was always someone there with me who had that red and black parka that you used to be able to get for free by redeeming Marlboro Miles.

2002: AN INTERNET ODYSSEY

The story of technology is also the story of the evolution of humiliation.

I was a "late adopter" of the internet. I finished high school in 1994, in one of the last graduating classes to not use the internet in any way in the classroom. The little exposure I had involved futzing around Courtney Love and Bikini Kill Angelfire fansites, at my techy friend Dave's house, while he hovered over my shoulder, to make sure I didn't break anything. In late 2000, when my mother bought me a WebTV she'd seen advertised in *Parade*, The New York *Times* Sunday supplement magazine, it was my first real independent exploration of the web. It was just me, my keyboard and screen, and my little orange bottle of 2 milligram Xanax.

I spent a considerable amount of my time online drooling on myself, arguing with the Courtney Love haters who camped out on her website, and searching for low-effort ways to get off the pills. None existed. The options were always the same: tapering from the Xanax slowly, or switching to a longer acting benzodiazepine, like Klonopin. My internet interests tag-teamed themselves one day when Courtney logged into the site, and gave me advice on how to get off the pills herself: *Go to the doctor*, she wrote. *And never, ever, mix them with opiates. Oh well!* I thought to myself. *Too late!* My post to thank her looked like this: *I l;ovvde ytttou soo fruckiolngf m;ucgh!* Her post to me looked like this: *Gtio tfo thE docxtoikr.*

Procuring and ingesting Xanax had become my life, and I stopped going out with my friends in New York City. Before giving up on sociality, I had been seeing a filmmaker named Hans. It was no great love affair, but had gone on for over a year, and when I disappeared, he noticed. He sent a message to my WebTV email address: He'd joined an online journal community, he wrote. It was still in its infancy, and in order to sign up, you had to be invited by someone who already had an account. I didn't really understand, but clicked on the link he'd sent. It took me to a website called livejournal.com and told me to create a journal name. After five seconds of deep intellectual contemplation, I came up with one that I thought was funny: crackpipe. I clicked over to Hans's LiveJournal, and quickly scrolled through his posts to see if he had written anything about me. He had. I had been after a mutual friend of ours, a singer in a band named Frank, before going dark. It hadn't really gone anywhere, because Frank's friends all thought I was bad news, because I was on drugs. In Hans's LiveJournal, he had written about seeing me at one of Frank's shows, where I'd been nodding out near the stage. I was "the new Nancy Spungen," he wrote. *As if!* I thought to myself. I considered replying, but couldn't figure out how.

I was able to glean from reading Hans's LiveJournal that he had been seeing someone new, an artist and writer named Rachel whose name I recognized from posters I'd seen advertising her one-woman plays around the Lower East Side. She also had a LiveJournal. I wasn't exactly jealous, my relationship with Hans no longer involved those kinds of feelings, but I was intrigued by the strange new access to people's lives that LiveJournal offered. Here was my ex-beau's new girlfriend, and I could read all about her, and their relationship, from what they wrote about it. Or at least I *could* have read those things: My WebTV was cut off a few days after I set up my journal. I couldn't pay my phone bill.

⁊

Fast forward, a year later: New York City had become a giant milk carton, with photos of the missing, and the soon to be confirmed dead, everywhere. I will never forget walking through Grand Central Terminal, and seeing all those photos, all those faces, and knowing most of them were gone. The flyers were all over the city, but at Grand Central they were more organized. It was like walking through a Lost and Found for people.

One morning, in early October 2001, I was nodding out on a bench in Tompkins Square Park when a woman with a European accent spat on the ground next to my feet, and said it was because of people like me that New York City was being attacked. I came out of my stupor long enough to jump up from where I was sitting and kick her hard in the ass. By December, I had fold-out posters of American flags from *The Daily News* blocking out the light that shined into my apartment through my bedroom windows. My dogs hid from me. By January, I'd lost my apartment.

When I arrived at my mother's house in Connecticut, I was taking twenty 2 milligram bars of Xanax a day. It had been an insane amount of medication to stay on top of. The maximum dosage a corrupt for pay doctor (or "croaker") in New York would prescribe for me was for 2 milligrams of Xanax four times a day, so I'd started taking Klonopin, the longer-acting benzodiazepine of internet lore, too. I had four doctors in New York City: I would see each of them once a month, or more than once a month, the times I could afford to pay them to act convinced when I said I'd lost my pills, or had them stolen. There were also a few people I could buy from, in a jam, in and around my methadone clinic.

Yes, I was also on methadone. This is what made Courtney Love "too late," with her advice about the opiate-mixing.

Maybe I could have continued the madness for a little bit longer if I hadn't moved in with my mother, in the boonies, and knew how to drive a car, but I'd moved in with my mother, in the boonies, and didn't know how to drive a car. As soon as I got to her house, she took me to the emergency room so I could be farmed out to a local doctor, and try to get my prescriptions transferred.

The doctor at the ER guffawed.

"This is insane!" he said. "Criminal! You are 25 years old! We are getting you off these pills!"

I checked into a detox center. I got off the methadone. I mostly got off the pills. In 2002, drug detoxes were still hesitant about treating benzodiazepine dependency: it was a long-term detox, with a high risk for seizures. I got down to 1 milligram of Klonopin, three times a day. I was blessed in that living with my mother offered me a slight grace period: I didn't have to find a job right away as long as I attended an outpatient drug treatment program. I started having these weird twinges of self-esteem. I wanted the people I'd known in New York City to remember that I existed, but I didn't feel ready to actually face them. Was there a middle ground? There was. The internet. I messaged livejournal.com and retrieved my long-forgotten "crackpipe" password.

❧

How Should a Person be, on the Internet?

In 2002, my answer to this question would have been *a lot like Courtney Love, on the internet*. A person should be smart, with a good vocabulary, a "machination" thrown in here or there, or a reference to Grand Guignol theatre, but these smarts did not necessarily have to be communicated by way of good grammar and spelling. (These stylistic licenses should be tolerated by the audience, because, in a sense, they were artistic, and non-conformist.) A person should be funny on the internet, in a quirky, self-effacing way, with lots of little digs lobbed at the self for being such a fuck-up. (*I am enjoying even this downward dance*, to quote Colum McCann, the little digs should imply.) A person should know a lot about fringy, outsider-type artists, especially those who have died by misadventure, and post lots of links and videos about them in memoriam. A person should "live loudly" on the internet: nothing about their personal life should be off limits.

In their LiveJournal, a person should write about their sex life in cringe-inducing detail. And on March 2, 2002, a person should post a LiveJournal entry that implies that while they were working as an escort in New York City, they fucked Mick Jagger, who first twisted their thong into a deep wedgie, flirtatiously, in the laundry room of a made-up friend's luxury apartment. A person should believe they are crafting their myth, on a server, for future generations to find. *So help them God.*

A person, when reintroducing themselves to people who they have not seen for a while, because their life went down the tubes, should definitely be hot on the internet. This should be accomplished by posting pictures of yourself, looking hot, to your LiveJournal.

There is not a more efficient, one-stop way of announcing to the world that you are back and on your A-game than posting a good photo of yourself online. Nowadays, this is too easy: grab your phone, smile or scowl, depending upon your worldly perspective, and your smartphone settings can post it for you. In 2002, the word "selfie" had only a masturbation connotation. To take a picture of yourself, and post it on the 'net, you needed a web cam.

My drug treatment program took up four hours of my day. I spent the rest of my time fucking around online, writing in my LiveJournal, or reading the LiveJournal's of others. Both Hans and Rachel updated theirs frequently, and after reading more of Rachel's, I discovered that she was smart, funny, an excellent writer, an amazing artist, and doing basically all of the things that I had moved to New York City to do, but never did, mostly because I was always running around chasing drugs. All that I had squandered while living in New York hit me with every one of her posts. I wanted to be a contender, too. I wrote in my LiveJournal about the books I was going to write. One would be entitled *Cope Sickness*. (Clever!) Another, *The Klonopin Diaries*. (Even more clever!) But these books, if I ever logged out of LiveJournal to get to work and start writing them, would take time. And focus. A good picture — being hot — was something I could do *now*, only I didn't have a web cam. Having a good picture to post of myself on LiveJournal began to feel more and more imperative.

Since I was presenting myself on the site in a loud and brash way, I thought nothing of commenting on Hans's journal to ask him about Rachel, even though she could see and read everything that I wrote.

"So, Rachel's an artist," I wrote. "But is she really 'talented'?"

"Yes, I'm an artist," Rachel responded. "But why did you put quotes around 'talented'?"

"Because 'talented' was always Hans word for 'hot,'" I wrote, feeling like I was schooling her on something.

"Yes," Hans answered. "She's one of the most 'talented' women I've ever met."

But I already knew this. Rachel had pictures of herself on her LiveJournal page. She obviously had a web cam.

&

Hans and Rachel had been working on a low-budget movie together that Rachel had written. This bothered me. It bothered me, because for a brief, shining moment, I had wanted to do something with film. It was one of the reasons I'd moved to New York, one of the reasons I'd gotten involved with Hans, but he was always dismissive of my ideas. What was different about Rachel? Why had he taken her ideas seriously, but not mine?* Though they were able to work together creatively, their relationship was by no means smooth. Hans was an inveterate cheat, and a few days before the premiere of their movie, an angry Rachel posted in her LiveJournal that Hans had ditched her at a bar, to go and canoodle with the daughter of a notorious underground film star.

---

*now the answer is abundantly clear to me: Hans was a dick, and I was on drugs.

"Ugh," a friend of hers named Newport Craig commented underneath her post.

"Fucking asshole," Rachel wrote. "I wish I could twist it in a way that would make people more interested in seeing our movie, but when you're as OLD as Hans is, the only 'stars' that want to fuck you are the three-degrees-removed, nepotistic, nobody-cares-kind."

Whenever she posted about their problems, I'd think about all the dickheaded things Hans had done or said to me, and how I'd always just sucked it up. Once, he'd left me waiting for him outside an after-hours bar at 6 o'clock in the morning. The bartender told me he'd left with another girl, but I'd refused to believe her, since he'd told me to wait. "You're a fucking asshole!" I said, finally getting him on the phone, later that afternoon. He didn't even try to deny that he'd left with the girl. He didn't try to justify himself in any way, at all. Instead, he'd said to me, *"Don't you ever talk to me like that again."* At the time, I'd still been in awe of him, and what I thought was his talent. I didn't want our relationship to end. So I didn't talk to him that way again — *ever*. Eventually, I wouldn't care enough about our relationship to talk to him that way, and expel the emotion.

But I loved that Rachel *did*. What had started off as curiosity, then envy of her talents, had morphed into sincere admiration.

The movie that Rachel and Hans had made together was released, and was a success. They posted pictures from its opening night on LiveJournal. His association with her made him more palatable to people as an artist, cuddlier, if that was possible: his persona as a downtown filmmaker had always been based on a certain kind of 80s New York City nihilism. But he must have had reservations, and felt that his rep was something he needed to uphold. A few days after the premiere, Rachel and Hans had another fight, and Rachel posted in her journal, "He wouldn't put his name on the film until after we did a screening. Up until the last minute, when he saw how much people liked it. Fucking asshole."

❧

I was not the only person on LiveJournal without a web cam: A lot of people didn't have them, and this was often reflected in their choice of user photo. Not having an actual picture of themselves to use, people used images from the web of things they felt represented them. My user photos were of Hollywood Madam Heidi Fleiss and Father Dougal McGuire from the popular '90s RTE show, *Father Ted*. *Father Ted* was a comedy sitcom about three Irish-Catholic priests exiled by their parish to the fictional Craggy Island for being fuckups. The title character, Father Ted Crilly, had criminal inclinations, and harbored fantasies of being a gambler, and a rock star. Father Jack Hackett used crude language, and was an alcoholic womanizer. Father Dougal McGuire was the wide-eyed naïf, a Baby Huey type, who recited Madonna's "Papa Don't Preach" at bedtime because he couldn't remember his prayers. By switching between his photo and Heidi's, I was basically communicating to everyone on the site that I was a sexually charged idiot. And then my posting style backed it up.

Newport Craig's user photo was of a pencil sketch drawing of a pensive looking man sitting on a tree branch that had originally run as a cartoon in the *New Yorker*. I don't know. Maybe it was because it was a pencil sketch. Maybe it was because it was a pencil sketch from the *New Yorker*. Maybe it was the "Newport" in his user name. I imagined, taken as a whole, this meant in real life he was preppy, and literary.

Newport Craig was someone who posted a lot in Rachel's LiveJournal, and in the LiveJournal's of other fringy New York artists. After a few months of reading her posts, my feelings about Rachel had morphed still further. I projected onto her. In my head, I saw her as a kind of New York City folk hero. Not only did she stand up to the big meanie Hans whenever he acted like a dickhead, she stood up for New York City in her writing, rebuking Rudy Giuliani and his post-9/11 pose as "America's Mayor."

When I saw Newport Craig's posts in Rachel's journal, and Rachel's posts in his, I interpreted it as a "vouch." If Rachel knew Craig, and liked him, he needed no other character witness. So when he posted in his LiveJournal that for his 40th birthday he wanted nothing more than to be photographed naked, surrounded by a group of equally-naked females, I thought to myself, *this sounds like an opportunity.*

Does this mean you have a web cam? I messaged him. When he responded in the affirmative, I told him I'd come to his apartment on his birthday, and let him photograph me naked, if he'd email me copies of the pictures. I wanted to post them in my LiveJournal.

ೞ

I don't know if showing up at a stranger's house to be photographed naked so I would finally have "hot" pictures to post is the crowning horror of my 2002 online year. There are too many contenders to choose from. The implied-Mick Jagger laundry room sex post is one. There's a "Virtues of Anal Sex" post that is so graphic that there is almost a scratch and sniff element to it. (Newport Craig commented on the post, to tell me he "liked my style.") In 2003, my online role model, Courtney Love, would let a stranger (who the media would describe as "a homeless man") suck her nipple outside of a Wendy's Restaurant. Maybe it was the *Girl's Gone Wild* vibe in the air, combined with our punk rock backgrounds, combined with our drug use (though I was on a lot less drugs than I had been the year before) that made these *displays* seem like good ideas to us at the time. It's all so shameless, and the worst kind of shameless: the empathetic, guilt-transference kind. The kind of shameless where you, the audience, if you are a compassionate person, end up feeling so bad for the person who can't be shamed that you take on their shame for them. And when that person is actually you, fifteen years ago... This is what it feels like when I read my LiveJournal now. I feel so bad for this person. And this person is me.

☙

Around this time, my posts on LiveJournal became too much for Hans. Though he was an artist in the "no boundaries" vein, I think what I wrote in my journal embarrassed him because people on the site knew about our past association. We'd been arguing online, about stupid stuff, and one day I snapped back at him (maybe to make up for the times during our relationship when I didn't?) and called him out by his real name, not the name he used on the site, and as a filmmaker. "You are the biggest asshole I've ever met," he wrote. "Wow," I responded. "The biggest? At 70 years old," I wrote, making fun of his age, like Rachel did when they fought, "You must have met a lot of assholes!" Then he unfriended me on the site, and banned me from posting in his journal.

This meant he would probably not get to see my "hot" photos, when I posted them.

☙

I still do this sometimes — find myself wanting attention so badly when I'm online, that I'm tempted to remove an article or two of my clothing, and post a picture. Only now this impulse is tempered by the awareness that whatever attention I get is not going to be the attention I want. The people whose attentions I might enjoy directed towards my body will not respond; it will always be the people whose attentions I don't want who will. But I've had to learn this the hard way, like everything. And I still have to remind myself. Attention is a drug, and sometimes, I want to abuse it.

თ

Newport Craig and I messaged a bit about logistics: where he lived, and what subway stop was closest to his house. He was still trying to line up other ladies to get naked, because for his birthday, his dream was to be surrounded by a bevy of naked ladies, as if to imply by the sheer number of bodies that the interest in him was not some fluke. Though I had envisioned Newport as being cute, despite what would be our mutual nakedness, I didn't want, or even consider, anything sexual happening between us. I just wanted the pictures. I could have given a shit about it being his birthday. I wasn't a friend jumping out of a cake for him. I didn't know him at all. Another thing that bothers me about this now is that it never occurred to me to ask him for money. Though I never had sex with Mick Jagger, I'd been a sex worker. I knew better.

თ

I called Craig from a payphone as soon as I exited the subway. He lived in a nice area, and obviously enjoyed a degree of financial security. When he met me at the door of his building, I was surprised by his appearance. Your mind makes leaps in the online realm, based on the information that's available to you, and I'd assumed he'd be more... *something*? Leading up to "the big day," he'd started referring to the pictures we'd be taking as "making art," like a greasy salesperson, trying to upsell a shady product. He looked like an uncle, any uncle, like one of the numerous, interchangeable, faceless men who I'd see making themselves a coffee with non-dairy creamer at an AA meeting. He wasn't bad looking, just totally non-descript. He was obviously nervous. I wasn't. I was all business (albeit bad business). There was another woman there, an ex-girlfriend of his, who he said had agreed to be in the photos as a favor to him. If that was true, it was kind of a strange favor, so I imagine that she must have still had feelings for him, which is a testament to his character: It means to someone, he was lovable. He was wearing a robe, like the cliché idea of Hugh Hefner, or maybe it was purely functional, because he'd soon be removing it. He said he wanted to take the photos in front of the fireplace, like we were making a Christmas card. Then Rachel arrived. I hadn't known for sure she was going to be there, though Newport had said that she might be. He would later write about this day in his LiveJournal in detail. In his minute by minute account of the 20 minutes that it took, he would describe me as a "ravishing blonde, clad in East Village attire." The end part of his description of me is what initially struck me about Rachel. She was wearing a long, '70s *Partridge Family* style dress that looked like it came from a thrift store. She and I didn't really talk much. What could I say? *How's Hans? Does he still think I'm the biggest asshole he ever met?* I've always been better at fan-girling from afar, because for me, so much of it is about the projection. No one can live up to my hype. I'd made plans to meet up with the person who was my last real contact in New York before I'd lost my apartment, an older guy who I always got high with. I'd decided since I was going to be in the city, I was going to get really fucking high. As we were milling around waiting for Newport to set up the camera, I heard Rachel say to him, "Hans cannot find out about this. If you post the pictures in your journal, you cannot post any with my face or any identifying details." I was surprised that Rachel would ever feel the need to hide anything from anyone.

Then we all took our clothes off and I saw that Rachel and I were groomed in the exact same way that women who have shared boyfriends sometimes are. When Newport wrote about the actual picture-taking in his journal, he wrote that I jutted my leg out around his arm (he was kneeling on the floor in front of us), the implication being that I had wanted him to touch me *there*.

Gross.

℗

So here we are at the great denouement: What happened when I posted the pictures online. Was it worth it? Was it all that I imagined it would be, and more?

Newport had taken the pictures with a timer, so we were all jammed together in what he'd predetermined to be an appropriate amount of space. The three of us stood behind him, with him in front, on his knees. Because Rachel had said she didn't want to be identifiable in any of the photos, Craig edited them in some kind of primitive Photoshop that covered the tattoos on her stomach and arms with pictures of his cat. Since I'd been standing next to Rachel, I had the tail of the cat that he'd superimposed across her stomach curling out and onto my stomach. For Rachel's benefit, he also cropped off all of our heads. Since he was kneeling, his face and chest were visible, with essentially, three women's headless bodies with cats jutting across two of them. When I asked him to send me the unedited photos, he said he couldn't, because of the risk to Rachel's "anonymity." He said he would re-crop them. I told him to keep the ones of all of us, and just send pictures of me. He sent me a close up of my upper body. I'd been decapitated again. Finally he sent me a picture that I thought I could use, but it was not at all what I'd been expecting — it had originally been a picture of his ex-girlfriend and me, but he'd cropped her out. It was of the upper part of my body, my chest, but at least I had a head. My hair was blonde at the time, like Craig had written in his journal, but I didn't look "ravishing." I'd worn a hat for some reason, and had my hair in Swiss Miss-style wrap around braids. In the photo, my hands were resting on my torso, and I was looking off to the side. I looked like a Rubenesque Norwegian.

Still I posted it. I really think I thought I had a shot at crashing the site.

But no one commented a thing.

A LiveJournal user named Larry left a comment on an older post of mine, about the death of Dee Dee Ramone.

"Did you see my new picture?" I asked him.

"Yes," he responded. "How could I miss it? It's sure to cause you a world of grief, crackpipe. Hope it's what you want!"

☙

I had about 50 "friends" on LiveJournal. In real life, I knew about ten of them, mostly peripherally, through Hans. Nobody I knew while living in Connecticut was on the site, nor did I invite anyone I knew there onto it. While I can't say I did this deliberately, I did do it purposefully. I didn't want anyone in my day to day life to be able to question, attempt to corral, or critique what I posted. I wanted no checks and balances; no accountability. I wanted the absolute freedom to make a fool of myself, and I did.

The crackpipe journal still exists. I no longer use it, and have since made great swaths of it private. I can't believe some of things that I wrote. I want to say it was drugs, but I put it out there. I craved the attention. I view it now as my internet adolescence, and it makes me so grateful that I had my actual flesh and blood adolescence in a pre-internet world.

There is a scene in the Werner Herzog documentary *Grizzly Man*, about the life and death of Timothy Treadwell, a self-styled animal conservationist who went and lived amongst the wild bears of Alaska, and was eventually killed, and eaten by the bears there. After listening to the audio recording Treadwell's video camera made of his death, Herzog tells Treadwell's friend that she shouldn't listen it. "*You must never listen to this, ever,*" he says. I feel a similar way when I attempt to read through my LiveJournal now.

You must never do that ever again.

CALIFORNIA DREAMING

When the man on the phone said he was a cop, I wasn't quick to believe him. We'd had excommunicated family members and abusive ex-boyfriends try similar ruses before, hoping to get information out of less suspicious staff members.

"Could you fax us something official from your police department?" I asked.

"Um... Could you hold on? I'm not really sure how... Um, let me ask my secretary."

He put the phone down and I could hear papers shuffling in the background. Even if the fax machine was a stretch, I figured a real police officer would at least know how to use a hold button.

He returned to the line. "OK. It's important that someone gets in touch with me ASAP. Her body is at the morgue, and we have no idea who to contact in the way of next of kin."

As he was talking, my call waiting went off. While his phone number had registered as "caller unknown," I could see on the caller ID that it was my boss, Lisa.

"Hold on for a minute," I said, feeling a bit strange that I was telling a potential lawman what to do.

Even with my boss's permission, my access to client information was limited. My weekend job at the halfway house involved no contact with the client files, and I had no access to the locked filing cabinet that housed them. As I explained the situation to Lisa, it was clear she didn't feel compelled to come down to the house and unlock the cabinet. To compound matters, she was on vacation, and wouldn't be back to work 'til the middle of the week.

"We have her phone number in that Christmas card she sent us above the desk," she said. "You can give that to him."

I switched lines.

"That was my boss. She said she'll fax you the contact information we have on Wednesday. She did say that I could give you a phone number that we have for Christine."

"640-6757?" he asked.

"Yes."

"That's her boyfriend's number. He doesn't know anything, besides leading me to you guys."

At that moment his fax came through. The heading on it read, *Detective Sergeant Paul Jones, Norwich Police Department.* Quickly, I tried to remember what Christine had told me about her life, but we had so many different women coming through the house that their background stories tended to blur. Often, it was only the dramatic circumstances surrounding their discharges that lingered.

"What happened to her?" I asked.

"We're not sure. Her boyfriend said she had been having a hard time breathing. He went out, and when he came back, he found her in the bathroom."

"I'm sorry I couldn't help more," I said, hanging up the phone.

Alone with my thoughts, I could see Christine, in life.

She was in the staff office, and I was giving her her morning meds, an abnormally large Ziploc freezer bag filled with various non-narcotic prescriptions. It was going to take her a little while to get all the pills out of their individual bottles, so she pulled a chair over from the computer to sit down. Christine was morbidly obese, and even small acts like opening pill bottles were labor intensive.

It was the dog days of summer, and she was wearing a bright blue muumuu tank dress. Though commodious enough for her girth, the dress was too short, and stopped right above her knees, giving full display of her swollen, lobster-red ankles. Her furry bedroom slippers spoke of comfort, an impossible offering to the painfully inflated flesh cleaved inside them. A few days after she had arrived at the halfway house, Lisa had forced her to cut off some cheap plastic bracelets because her arms had swelled purple underneath them. She had fought what had initially just been a suggestion, saying she enjoyed the tingling sensation. If she couldn't smoke crack anymore, she said, she should at least be allowed the pleasant feeling that the blockage of her blood flow provided.

I worked at a halfway house for the treatment of drug addiction issues. I worked on the weekends, when there was no program time, and the women could do whatever they wanted, as long as it was drug and alcohol-free, and respected the 12AM curfew. I never spent that much time with Christine because on the weekends while I was there, she slept all day. Often, when I'd be giving her her morning meds, it would no longer be morning, but close to 5PM.

"So tell me about yourself, Chrystal," I said, initializing the boxes for each prescription on her med sheet. "Number one, what is the deal with your name?"

On all of her paperwork, her name was listed as *Christine*, but she insisted that everyone at the house call her *Chrystal*.

She smiled, and the swells of her cheeks retreated higher up the framework of her face. "I'm just more of a *Chrystal* than a *Christine*," she said. She had a Big Gulp cup in front of her, and washed her pills down with house Kool-Aid that stained her mouth blue. "I like crystals and believe in their healing power. I used to follow the Grateful Dead, and got the nickname on Dead tour. Have you ever seen my Jerry bear dance?"

She lifted her arm, and revealed a red dancing bear tattooed on the underside of it. She tapped the loose skin in area of the tattoo, and the bear's arms and legs appeared to move as her skin swung back and forth like a fleshy pendulum.

"Where did you grow up?" I asked.

"Mass., mostly. That's where my adoptive parents lived. But I was made in *Cali-forn-ia*. That's where my birth mother lived at the time." She relayed this information with a dreamy quality to her voice. "Someday, I'll get back there. I'm a Cali girl at heart, though it's been awhile since I've been home. I think the last time was

Dead Tour, '92? My boyfriend calls me *Hollywood*. I hate having to take these Big Pharma meds. I prefer alternative therapies. Herbs, Reiki."

"Do you know your birth parents?" I asked.

"No, but my adoptive parents met my mother. She was a big girl, too. Growing up, I was a big Mamas and the Papas fan. You know, the folk group? I always felt this *connection*. I read that Cass Elliot put a child up for adoption a few years before she died. It makes sense, with my age and everything. I read that the daughter Joni Mitchell put up for adoption heard *Ladies of the Canyon* and just knew that Joni was her mom. My adoptive parents tried to convince me otherwise, but it's not like they would have recognized Cass. They're big squares."

"Have you seen your birth certificate?"

"That doesn't mean anything. Cass wouldn't have had to use her name."

She pricked her finger to get her blood sugar reading and began preparing her insulin.

"For Halloween this year — I'm a pagan and I love All Hallows' Eve — I'm going to be Cass. I'll sing for my candy. *California Dreaming on such a winter's day!*"

"You should watch the candy with your diabetes."

"Oh, I will. Whatever I get, I'll donate it to the kids at the Women's Center."

Christine hadn't been popular with the other women living at the halfway house. One of the reasons involved her actions in relation to the house's food supply. She hoarded everything, from ketchup packets to teabags, to once, a whole family-sized rotisserie chicken. The halfway house had a communal eating arrangement, but when the groceries came for the week, Christine would furtively grab whatever she could, and hide it in her room. *Whatever she could* cut into the idea of equal distribution significantly. Clients were not allowed to have food upstairs in their rooms, and she'd been caught many times with perishable and non-perishable food items hidden in drawers, and under her bed.

Most of the time, she tried to blame her roommate, Janice.

"It was Janice!" Christine would say. "She did it! She wants me gone so she'll have the room all to herself! She knew you'd all believe her, over me, because I'm fat!"

The women also made complaints about Christine's hygiene. They said she never showered, and when she used the bathroom, it required "fumigation" afterward. It wasn't the kind of complaint Lisa normally took seriously, until she used the bathroom after Christine. Quietly, she took her aside, and pointed out the air freshener kept under the sink, but Christine refused to use it, saying it contained dangerous chemicals.

Lisa ordered her to spray it or go on house restriction.

Summer became fall as my scant memories of Christine moved forward in time. It was a few months later, and she was back in the office, taking her pills. She'd been sleeping all day, because what else was there for her to do? she said. She was on house restriction, again, for having food in her room. She would not be able to go out for Halloween as Cass Elliot, because Halloween fell over the restriction period.

She blamed the holiday for the food found in her room this time.

She told Lisa that the ham slices in plastic wrap found under her bed were part of her Mama Cass costume.

Lisa, unfamiliar with the urban legend surrounding the death of the folk singer, looked at Christine incredulously, and asked her what her Halloween costume had to do with hiding food.

"That's how Cass *died*," Christine said. "She choked on a ham sandwich. I was going to make a big one, and carry it with me."

In the staff office, a big *R* for restriction was next to Christine's name on the board that served as the client roster.

A few minutes into her pill-taking, Christine was still out of breath from her trip down the stairs. When she finished, she said she was going back up to her room to finish her nap before major cleaning. I watched as she ascended the stairs slowly, with much effort.

Every Sunday, the halfway house was cleaned thoroughly. Each client had a job to do. That week, Christine had an easy one — the small downstairs bathroom. Though major cleaning lasted two and a half hours to allow time for the bigger jobs, like the cleaning of the kitchen and the basement, Christine's job could have been done, and done well, in fifteen minutes.

Assigned chores happened in rotation — having an easy one one week meant the next week's job would be more involved and time-consuming.

Despite the ease of her assignment, Christine did a horrible job. It appeared she had just changed the toilet paper roll and deemed herself finished.

I found her upstairs in bed, and brought her back down to the bathroom. By giving her a chance to do it again, I was being generous. Another staff member would have just added time to her restriction.

As the order of chores went, next she would be in charge of the kitchen, and I anticipated it would be a nightmare. The women would demand she wear gloves when cooking house meals, and the clean up afterward: I foreshadowed dirty pans washed without soap, then hidden under the sink, until it was time to prepare the next night's meal.

The last time I saw Christine, she came into the office after seeing the next week's chore list.

"If I can find someone to agree to switch the kitchen with me, can I?" she asked.

"No, Chrystal. You can't trade chores unless you have a job, and will be at work. You know this," I said.

That night, Christine confided to Janice that she'd thought she'd come up with a way to get out of her turn doing the house's most daunting task. If it all played out the way she hoped, not only would she not have to cook and clean, she would get a break from the monotony of house life. She would get to sleep all day — something that wasn't allowed at the house Monday through Friday — and have her meds and meals delivered to her in bed. She would also be able to talk to her boyfriend on the phone in her room.

She gave Janice five dollars to watch her belongings, and apologized for blaming the hidden food on her so many times.

"I figured they'd give you an easier time about it than me," she said. "People are always meaner to the big girl."

When she woke up the next day, Lisa was working. Christine went into the staff office and asked her in a calm voice to please call 911. She was hearing voices, she said. They were telling her to hurt herself.

She called Lisa a few days later from the psych ward, to check in with her, and tell her how she was feeling.

"The doctor says I'm stabilized and can come back to the house next week," she said cheerfully.

Lisa, informed of Christine's scheming by Janice, who had considered five dollars to be an insulting bribe, decided to skip the lecture.

"Sorry, hon, but we've given your bed away. I've talked to your case manager, and he's looking into alternative arrangements for you."

"Well...what about all my stuff?" Christine asked.

"It's safe, hon. It's in the basement. Come and get it when you can. And feel better."

Lisa said that while Christine sounded surprised, she didn't seem particularly angry.

As I remembered what Lisa said, I looked up at the Christmas card that was tacked to the wall of the office, and contained the phone number I had tried to give to Detective Jones.

Inside the card, Christine had written:

Happy holidays/ Io, Saturnalia!
Miss you guys!
Love, Chrystal E.

While Christine had been living at the halfway house, her last name had begun with a *G*. Lisa thought she might have gotten engaged to her boyfriend: she thought his last name was something like "Earle."

I decided that the *E* was for "Elliot." Maybe in the last few months of her life, Chrystal had found a small way to realize her California dream.

I got up from the desk and pulled on the filing cabinet drawer. I was surprised when it opened. I decided to take my chances with Lisa's anger. I found Christine's folder, and called Detective Jones.

GHOUL GIRL GROWS UP

It was my father who first got me interested in all things Charles Manson. As a young girl, I was attention starved, and impressionable. One morning, while my dad was sitting across from me at the breakfast table, I took my napkin from my lap, and placed it on my head. "Look dad, I'm a napkinhead!" I laughed with glee, hoping to win his attention away from the Sunday paper. "You look like Squeaky Fromme," he grunted, and went back to his reading.

Squeaky Fromme? Who was she? I hoped only the most glamorous woman in the entire universe. Did I always look like her, or just with the napkin? I wondered.

"Dad, who's Squeaky Fromme?"

And so it began: the question that would eventually lead me to buy at least ten different copies of the book, *Helter Skelter*, because whenever my mother found the book in my bedroom, she'd throw it out. Squeaky, who was no stranger to the media, had been in and out of the news, mostly as a punch line, because of her half-hearted attempt to shoot President Ford. While most in Manson's group of vagabond hippies and LSD casualties had moved on, no longer wanting to be associated with what had gone on in and around Los Angeles in August of 1969, Squeaky was still willing to admit with pride to her active involvement in what was left of Charlie's Family. Before the assassination attempt, she'd been acting as Charlie's de facto spokesperson. She said she'd pulled the gun on the president to bring attention to Manson's new crusade, an environmental group he'd started in prison, known as ATWA. Hence the napkin-resembling headgear: a sort of a eco-fabulous twist on the Hellenic head scarf with a secondary purpose — to keep the hair out of your eyes when you had a gun in your hands.

My mother came into the room, and my Manson family history lesson was cut short. But I was intrigued. I wanted to find out more about these murderous, desert- dwelling hippies, and their height-challenged leader. Besides appeasing my curiosity, it would be great for father-daughter relations, I reasoned, giving my dad and me something to talk about that interested us both.

My journey into all things Charles Manson soon took me to the library, a none too impressive small town affair. They didn't even have a copy of *Helter Skelter* which had been a monumental bestseller for its author, Vincent Bugliosi, the district attorney who had prosecuted Manson, Leslie Van Houten, Susan Atkins, and Patricia Krenwinkel. (Charles "Tex" Watson was also prosecuted by Bugliosi, but his trial was separate.) Slightly discouraged, but undaunted, I moved my search to the periodical files and found a treasure trove of original *Time* magazines covering the span of time from the Tate-LaBianca killings, to their convictions, and aftermath. Instead of just making copies, and leaving the magazines intact for future generations, I decided that these original articles should be mine alone, and ripped them out, placing them into a photo album that I designated my Manson Family scrapbook.

On a trip to Florida, I found what had so far been eluding me, a copy of the book *Helter Skelter*. As I entered the used book store, I remember feeling something go off inside of me, like a metal detector — a *Helter Skelter* detector. I knew that inside the store I would finally find a copy of my coveted book. I asked the person behind the counter to put it in a paper bag, like a forty ounce, so my mother wouldn't see it. Unlike my father, my interest in Charles Manson disturbed her. I'd recently changed my group of friends at school, and had started writing depressing poetry. I was smoking cigarettes, and had swapped the Monkees as my favorite band in favor of the Sex Pistols. My mother was concerned. One of the ways she dealt with her concern was to throw things away when she found them: my cigarettes, tapes, gloomy poetry, and anything Manson related.

I devoured *Helter Skelter* over that vacation. While my brother and sister splashed in the pool, I sat under a palm tree, and read court testimony. The book served as an outline for a host of new interests: I longed to try LSD, and did, as soon as the opportunity presented itself. I bought the Beatles *White Album* and poured over the lyrics. I read the New Testament, and familiarized myself with the Book of Revelation. Manson and his group started to shape my thoughts on relationships, and family: I yearned to find a group of people to accept me, and move to the desert with. I already suffered from 60s envy, having read about the dissident groups, and love-ins, and dreamed of uniting with other young people like myself, and living outside the status quo. Mine was an adolescence lived as an imaginary outsider, and Charles Manson was my cultural pariah of choice. But short of legal emancipation, I still had to finish school.

My parents had lived in New York City before having kids, and they'd take us on day trips there. It was on one of these excursions that I found what would become a staple of my high school wardrobe — a t-shirt proclaiming that I was a "Friend of the Family" in bold font, above a photo of Charlie, and a few of the girls. It went well with the Charles Manson shrinky dink bracelet that I'd traced and baked myself. During this time in the early 90s, a strange thing happened in mass marketing: serial killers became recognizable commodities, able to move product. Suddenly, it seemed like Manson was everywhere. Guns N' Roses covered Manson's songs. His face appeared on other musicians' album covers. A shock rock performer took "Manson" as his stage name, in combination with "Marilyn," a reference to Marilyn Monroe. Manson equaled "edgy" and popular culture wanted in on the association. I reacted the same way I would in the future when my favorite punk bands started to get famous — I backed away.

Charles Manson had sold out. It was time to move on, but I had my senior year thesis to do. I decided to write to Manson, and Leslie Van Houten, in the hopes that they'd start a correspondence with me. I had low expectations for Charlie. I knew he received hundreds of letters a week, but Leslie I thought was a real possibility. She was the Family member with the highest likelihood of parole, the one who, whenever her role in the murders was mentioned, was noted to have "stabbed someone who was already dead." With so much blood to go around, the splatter was residual, and there was still a high likelihood that she would spend her life in prison. I thought she might be receptive to the idea of communicating with a high school senior. Perhaps we would pass cautionary letters back and forth, bewaring the pitfalls of drugs, and peer influence, not only guaranteeing me an "A", but accolades for the inherent ambition of the project. These would be Geraldo caliber subjects communicating with me.

Neither wrote back. I did my thesis on the "Psychological Reasons Why People Follow the Grateful Dead." One of my bibliographical sources was a book by Courtney Love's crazy father.

℥

After graduating high school, I moved to New York City, and began a relationship with Chuck, a bassist whose brother had been a seminal punk rock musician known for his intimate knowledge of his own bodily fluids. Along with reissues of his deceased brother's music, Chuck sold and collected serial killer artwork. His art catalog included paintings by John Wayne Gacy, pen and ink designs by Danny Rolling, and watercolors by Henry Lee Lucas. Chuck explained to me that the murder memorabilia community was small, and that most of the dealers and collectors knew each other. Personal correspondence was also a big part of it, with collectors willing to spend hundreds of dollars for a letter authored by their preferred psychopath. When I mentioned to Chuck that I had written to Manson in high school, he laughed: Charlie mostly responded to young boys, thinking of himself as a father figure, and mentor to them, he said.

One day I was at Chuck's apartment when he got a phone call. He started talking about prices, and from what I could hear, appeared to be talking to two people at the same time. They agreed on a price for a drawing, and then Chuck started talking about me. I heard him say he thought I would be interested, and that he would pass along the person's address. "Yes," I heard him add cryptically, I "was hot."

It had been Richard Ramirez, and his wife, Darlene on the phone. Chuck had been dealing with Darlene for a while, giving her sums of money in exchange for "artwork" done by Ramirez — mostly skull and pentagram designs similar to what you might find on a high school head banger's notebook. Chuck would then resell the glorified creepy doodles to interested parties. Richard, known as "The Night Stalker," was on Death Row, which only increased the asking price for his work. It had been the same with John Wayne Gacy, and Ted Bundy, before they were executed. A sort of morbid, "get it while he's still hot" that made their works all limited editions, barring a commuted sentence.

"Richard wants you to write him." Chuck said. "If you write to him, he'll write you back."

I didn't know much about Richard Ramirez, outside of "The Night Stalker" sobriquet, and his heavy metal fixation. I knew he'd worn aviator sunglasses in the courtroom during his trial, and that he was on Death Row. I could remember seeing *Hard Copy* news footage after his sentencing; he told the camera he was "going to Disney World," and flashed a pentagram he'd drawn on his hand. In the news footage, he'd seemed borderline sentient, and like he was playing at being scary — a paint by numbers psychopath. It was as though he'd taken every early Ozzy Osbourne album as marching orders.

"What would I write to him about?" I asked Chuck. "I don't know anything about him."

"I don't know," Chuck replied. "Write about me. He doesn't write back to everyone. If they execute him, the letter's going to be worth money."

He scribbled out Richard's address, which included SAN QUENTIN in the city line, and his inmate number.

Later the night, I sat on my couch, with a paper and pen.

Dear Richard, I wrote.

This was going to be different from my letter to Charlie and Leslie, as I had no project to write about. I turned on the television as I struggled to come up with something to say. Why was I doing this? I did feel pressured a bit — any hesitation Chuck might have had about communicating with these types was abated by his love of the money it brought him. The title of a Lifetime movie starring Tori Spelling came into my mind: "*Mommy, Can I Sleep with Danger?*" My mother had consoled herself believing that I'd finally grown out of my ghoul girl phase. I told myself to relax — Richard Ramirez couldn't "get me." He was in a locked cell, on California's Death Row. But the details I was using to calm myself were the same reasons I should have been concerned. As I was sat conflicted, the popular Taco Bell commercial with the talking Chihuahua came on the television. *Yo quiero Taco Bell*, the little dog said. It gave me an idea. I had a roll of film that I'd recently developed of pictures of my own Chihuahua, Bridey.

> *Dear Richard,*
>
> *Hey. I'm the girl who's involved with Chuck. Hope all is well with you.*
>
> *Here's a picture of my Chihuahua, Bridey. Take care!*

Before I mailed the letter, I threw in a picture of Bridey, sunbathing on my Brooklyn rooftop, along with some stamps, which I knew to be a customary jail-house courtesy.

Time went by. My relationship with Chuck flamed out. He had a bit of a mean streak, as evidenced when my friend Penelope showed up outside his apartment after a big fight with her boyfriend, clad in only a long coat. Chuck didn't like Penelope, and nearly naked or not, refused to let her come up to his apartment. *Dames before lames*, I've always said, and never forgot his display of coldness. One night before the end of our relationship, I'd been at his apartment, and he'd asked me to put a movie on. He had shelves of videotapes lining the apartment's walls. The videos accurately reflected his interests — true crime, porn and punk music. He had the Richard Ramirez episode of the A&E investigative true crime series, *American Justice*. I decided to put it on, and learn a bit more about my potential pen pal.

After the first fifteen minutes, I didn't want to watch anymore. It was too much. A mother raped in front of her son, a gun held to the 12 year old boy's head. A husband killed in front of his wife, only luck allowing the woman to survive herself. Three cases of rape, murder, and mutilation of women over sixty, and the lingering question of what he had done with one of the woman's eyeballs. And that was only the beginning of the program.

Chuck didn't seem to be the least bit affected. He ate pizza, and made phone calls.

I felt terribly naive. I felt like I deserved to be scolded for being a silly, stupid girl. Could what I'd written to Ramirez be construed as a fan letter? Could it be interpreted as affirmation of what he'd done, or God forbid, support?

I reminded myself that I'd written him all of three lines, and sent him a picture of my Chihuahua. It was almost two months since I'd sent the letter, and he still hadn't written back.

And then he did. Chuck and I were over by then. I thought

about calling him, to have someone to share the experience with, but what was the experience? A moronic man, desperate for infamy, but with no skills to attain it but the cruel, senseless killing of vulnerable strangers, had sat in his cage and composed me a letter. I ripped open the envelope haphazardly — Chuck's face appeared in my mind with a scowl on it. Even envelopes were worth money.

Dear Fiona

Nice hearing from you. It takes about three weeks for me to get my letters. I like your dog, Bridey. Have you seen the Taco Bell commercial? Do you go into Manhattan a lot? Are you still with Chuck? Please send me pictures of you, I heard you are very pretty. Thanks for the stamps.

Your friend, Richard

I read it again, and unfolded the "likes and dislikes" form he'd inserted. It consisted of interview questions appropriate for a teen magazine — "favorite TV show," "favorite hobby," innocent, 'til you flipped it over, and the questions were all about sex: clearly, he had a foot fetish.

I became fixated on the closing: *Your friend, Richard.* I let it ruminate.

Well, Richard, I thought, *I'm not a very good friend. Maybe if we'd gotten to know each other a few years ago, it might have worked out.*

I thought of that line from the first Batman movie. Jack Nicholson, as the Joker, said it.

You ever dance with the devil in the pale moonlight?

Almost. I felt like I'd asked the devil to dance, but changed my mind as he reached for my hand.

KILLING ME SOFTLY:
ON ELLIOT RODGER AND THE POWER OF NO

On May 23, 2014, 22 year-old Elliot Rodger, the privileged son of a Hollywood filmmaker, went on a stabbing and shooting rampage in Isla Vista, California. Before taking his own life behind the wheel of his BMW 335is, Rodger killed six people, and left fourteen injured. Wanting to ensure that the impetus for his crimes would be clear to the world, Rodger sent out 107,000 word "manifesto," and uploaded a video to YouTube entitled "Elliot Rodger's Retribution." In the video, Rodger said:

Tomorrow is the day of retribution, the day in which I will have my revenge against humanity, against all of you. For the last eight years of my life, ever since I hit puberty, I've been forced to endure an existence of loneliness, rejection and unfulfilled desires all because girls have never been attracted to me. Girls gave their affection, and sex and love to other men but never to me…

You girls have never been attracted to me. I don't know why you girls aren't attracted to me, but I will punish you all for it. It's an injustice, a crime, because… I don't know what you don't see in me. I'm the perfect guy and yet you throw yourselves at these obnoxious men instead of me, the supreme gentleman.

Though "the supreme gentleman" killed both men, and women, Rodger referred to his plans as his "War on Women," his revenge on them for "starving" him of sex, leaving him a virgin.

℘

That "no means no" when it comes to sex has entered into mainstream thought as a concept; hopefully in a much more effective way than the last big no-should-be-enough campaign. That one just led to a lot of kids seeing Nancy Reagan's face in their weed the first time they smoked pot. But what about the smaller *nos* in the lives of women, and the consequences to us when we demur?

It was just my birthday, and as I typed to a man online who quickly made things personal when I declined to give him my home address so he could send me a present: *I'm tired of making concessions to things that make me uncomfortable.* I'm keenly aware as I write this that there will be people who will think that this is a pointless topic to contemplate. It's just an annoying fact of life, they will say, sometimes you say *yes* when you really want to say *no.* Often, it's a feelings-saving gesture or a societal politesse. But there's more to it than that. Sometimes, when no meets the male ego, the result is like the chemical reaction of combustibles. In the state where I live, a young girl was stabbed to death for saying *no* to a boy who asked her to the prom.

So far, I've been lucky in that I've only received emotional jabs not physical stabs as a result of my small *nos.* These jabs were mostly the ends of what I thought were real friendships with men. My mother's voice echoes through my head as I write this: "Well dear, those men were never your real friends anyway," and she would be right, but I think that what lies underneath what we've been dismissing as "suck it up, move on" non-events is a sentiment that should be acknowledged. There's an implication there.

Two years ago, I became friends with another writer on Facebook. Actually, seeing what I could of his profile at the time, I didn't even know that he was a writer. We had mutual friends on the site, including a female writer who is one of my heroes, and I used to see his posts on her page. From his profile picture, I saw that he chose to present himself to the world as a kitschy goofball; in the picture, he was wearing over-sized clown glasses, and a giant purple sombrero hat on his head. In his "About Me" section, I read that he had played in a band with a musician that I liked, so I sent him a friend request. Just another friend request, based on what I imagined would be our mutual interests. He accepted it, and began messaging me. Fairly soon afterward, he sent me an anthology he had a story in, with a cute inscription. I liked messaging with him. He wanted me to come to the city where he lived so we could meet, but I wasn't in any big hurry. I figured I'd probably run into him at a show or a reading someday. He kept asking me to call him on the phone, which was kind of annoying, but eventually I did, the first small *yes* when I would have preferred to say *no* that I made for our relationship.

Then, one weekend I was in his city, and agreed to meet up with him at a restaurant. It wasn't a date. It was an *I'm going to be near where you live, let's hang*. I was staying at a friend's apartment, and after so many shots at the bar, I decided it was time for me to go. As I was putting on my coat, he asked me if I wanted to go back to his apartment. With no set agenda for anything to do once we got there, the implication was pretty clear. *Did I want to go back to his place and engage in sexual activity?* No, I didn't, but I didn't say that. Instead, I went out of my way to stress how early I had to get up the next day. *It's not you, it's me,* I went out of my way to imply. *Don't think you're less of a stud. Think I'm a lightweight.*

The next morning, trying to be preemptive and stay a step ahead of any rejection-related weirdness he might have felt, I sent him a message asking if he wanted to get coffee before I went home. He typed back that he didn't, and that was it, effective immediately, our friendship was over. We are still connected via Facebook, but we do not communicate with each other at all anymore. He doesn't even say *Happy Birthday*, when everyone and their thrice removed cousin comes out of the woodwork on that site with an annual greeting. And there's my mother's voice again — and she's starting to get impatient: "Well, dear, he was never your friend."

Small *no* → consequence → suck it up → move on.

We aren't even supposed to ruminate on the endings of these "relationships." Nobody wants to hear it. It's just the way things go. We don't talk about the implication when a woman rejects a man, no matter how gently, and this is how he reacts. As a society, we will discuss it if his reaction is big — if it has a body count, but not if his reaction is bloodless. It is acceptable if he kills me in his mind, but not acceptable if he actually kills me.

I've watched about five minutes of Elliot Rodger's videos — it took me this long to finally sit down and force myself to do so — and I can tell after just watching those five minutes *why* women rejected him. Rodger's absolutely alienating, abrasive sense of entitlement: it drips from him. He doesn't even come across as human, but as a preening, posing set of entitlements and needs. Some kind of bitchy, alien anger baby. And he's not bad looking. He's well dressed and groomed. Some women like fancy cars, and he had one of those. But you can see that there is a disconnect there. He is a person who has grown up to believe just by the nature of his gender, that he is owed what he wants, and to not get what he believed he was entitled to, enraged him. He felt it was nothing less than an act of war to deny him what he felt was his birthright.

I felt bad about rejecting my "friend." I feel bad when I reject anyone. I've offered up convoluted excuses and complicated fabrications where an "I'm not interested" should have sufficed. And there have been times, depending on the man, where I've felt that I needed to tread as softly as possible when giving my small *no*, aware that there might be some kind of consequence. That my small *no* might not be the end of it. With the constant gains of technology, these consequences have become more nefarious. I have deleted men on Facebook and crossed my fingers that that would be the end of it. When I told the man on Facebook I would not give him my address so he could send me "my gift," he decided to give me what I'm sure in his mind was another kind of gift. He told me (in so many words) that I was rude, damaged, and obviously had trust issues that I needed to work on.

This isn't a polemic on empathy. I believe that the empathetic *no* is most women's default *no*, because somewhere along the lines we internalized it not just as a politesse, but as a survival tactic. Sometime in our lives, we either learned or observed that it was better to be careful with our small *nos*. The some men might react to them as if they were being attacked with a real weapon.

It's interesting to think, and not much of a leap, that if rape is about power, that it's predicated on the notion that our *no* is a weapon. Our freedom to choose, to decline, to demur, is seen by some as a power that we wield, and sexual assault is a way for men to take our power to say *no* away from us.

I chose the anecdote about my writer friend as an example because his "soft" killing of me stung a bit more than other times I have been killed in the minds of men over the past few years. I had hoped that he had taken me seriously as a peer, and the way our relationship ended proved that he had not. In my life, I haven't had that many experiences where I slept with a man, then never heard from him again. That's the stereotype: The woman wanting the emotional connection, and the man only being interested in the physical one. I have lost more relationships with men before we even got to that stage. I have lost more relationships with men because early on, I said *no* to them in some small way.

MY INNER DEBBIE GIBSON

I met Sam when I started working weekends at a women's halfway house. She was the "senior resident" (a fancy way of saying she was the client who had been there the longest), and had her own room, downstairs, next to the staff office. She was young, and energetic, and though the show wasn't on TV yet, bore a strong physical resemblance to Jenelle Evans from *Teen Mom*. She said she'd never forget the day I started working there. It was winter, and I'd come to the door wearing a purple knit hat. From then on, she said, she always thought of me whenever she heard the Prince song, "Raspberry Beret."

Sam had a lot of girlfriend drama in her life. She was a pretty, femme lesbian, and when we met, was involved in a stormy relationship with a married woman twice her age named Judy. The relationship was over one day, then the next, they were getting tattoos of each other's birthday dates between their shoulder blades. It was a relationship they both described as doomed, though they continued to do risk-heavy things, in defiance of the doom. Judy, who lectured Sam constantly about her irresponsible spending, still gave Sam an "emergency-only" credit card, while Sam planned on moving in with Judy and her husband, even though he hated her, when she left the halfway house.

Which she did one day, unexpectedly. She'd been on house restriction for coming home late. She and Judy had been arguing out in the driveway, and even though Sam had a watch on, and knew what time it was, she decided it was more important to stay outside and yell at Judy. The restriction was for a week, and she abided it for two long days. In AA and NA they talk about "hitting rock bottom" as the popular reason for seeking treatment, but it wasn't really true of Sam's situation. She'd come to the halfway house on the advice of a lawyer, after getting a second DUI. Drinking wasn't Sam's problem *per se*, it was more that she did everything in life recklessly, which in turn made her drinking a problem. When she left the halfway house, she didn't tell anyone. Instead, she left a note on her bed: *I'm outta hair like the bald man*, it said.

A few weeks later, she found me online, and sent me a message. *I want to keep in touch with you. I want to be your best friend*, she wrote. Her phraseology made me think of the Bikini Kill song, "Rebel Girl." *Sam wants to take me home, she wants to try my clothes on*. She was done with Judy. She had tried to force her into a threesome with her husband. She was staying with her dad, and wearing the same dress and underwear every day, because Judy refused to turn over her things, and had taken back the credit card.

I was glad to be back in touch with her. We'd talked a lot at the halfway house, and shared mutual interests. She preferred female artists, like I tend to, though when it came to music, she was into Ani DiFranco and Tori Amos, while I was into Lydia Lunch and Courtney Love. We both loved books. Cookie Mueller and Lisa Carver were my favorite writers, while V.C Andrews and Francesca Lia Block were hers. She wrote, too; reviews of big concerts, for a local paper, while I wrote poetry, and personal essays, mostly about the years I'd spent as a drug addict. As we became closer, she would say that the reason I wasn't interested in something "more" with her was that she wasn't "punk rock." She would say that the real difference between us was that she had never done heroin.

She made it clear that she would be interested in something "more" with me, but I wasn't going to date a former client of the halfway house. (For the sake of clarity, I'd describe my sexual orientation as "open to anything.") We went out for coffee a few times, but mostly followed each other's lives online. She was constantly meeting women there, over MySpace, and Facebook. It seemed like every week there was a picture of her with someone new, and a post that declared their affection for each other. When I asked about her sobriety, she told me she'd "cut wayyyyy back on the drinking, and was smoking a lot of weed." She posted pictures of herself and a love interest in bikinis, wearing backwards baseball hats, smoking blunts. I'm not a lecturer. I recommended she be cautious.

Then she met Jane. Jane was older, in her late forties, like Judy had been, her arms and hands covered in tattoos. Sam posted pictures of Jane doing shots off her stomach at Coyote Ugly, in New York City ("Jane drinks, but only sometimes," she messaged me), of her and Jane putting on helmets as they suited up to ride Jane's motorcycle. Things seemed to be getting serious in their relationship, then Sam got sick.

She posted pictures from the hospital, lying in a bed, with an IV in her arm. She posted pictures smiling when Jane came to visit, and wrote posts about missing her, when she felt she wasn't visiting enough. A few days later, Sam identified what had been ailing her in a detailed Facebook post.

A woman who I worked with at the halfway house named Liza, who knew Sam, and was also connected with her online, messaged me: *I can't believe she's posting about having a poop disease. A POOP DISEASE.*

Sam had been diagnosed with Inflammatory Bowel Disease at the hospital: Crohn's Disease.

While she was in the hospital, she called me. She was worried about her relationship with Jane. Her doctor said she needed to stop drinking once and for all, and the truth was, they went to bars and clubs *a lot*. Her prognosis was good — smoking pot was actually recommended. She viewed her diagnosis as a little bump in the road. If there was any silver lining, she'd lost the 15 lbs. she'd put on over the course of her relationship with Jane, but because Jane had liked her butt so much, this was also a concern.

Soon, she was out of the hospital, and posting pictures of her and Jane in Provincetown, on the beach. She looked blanched, and whisper-thin in her bikini. She messaged me that Jane was being *so understanding*: it turned out she'd had a serious illness herself when she was younger. But a few days later, Sam was back in the hospital. She'd been in horrible pain, and needed emergency surgery. A portion of her bowel had been rerouted through an opening made in her abdomen. This opening, known as a *stoma*, is for the release of bodily wastes normally handled by the colon. A pouch is attached to the stoma that must be emptied and cleaned throughout the day. The procedure is known as a colostomy.

I'd been shitting blood all week, she wrote to me. *I didn't want to tell Jane, but it got bad. As I was crapping my brains out in the bathroom, I was thinking that what Jane likes about me is that I'm young and sexy (LOL, you know I am). I don't feel very sexy right now.*

She needed help with her after-care when she released from the hospital. She moved in with her mom, an hour away from where Jane lived. Her mom tried to be accommodating, and said that Jane could sleep over. There was a three year age difference between Jane and Sam's mom.

Jane and I had been talking about getting a place, Sam wrote to me. *I hope I'm being paranoid, but it seems like she's being hedgy about that now.*

I have watery shit in a bag near my hip. I have watery shit in a bag near my hip. I wondered if the message was supposed to be a poem, or rap lyrics. *My gun is a colostomy bag.* My bullets are shit. I wondered if Sam was drinking, or abusing her pain meds, but she was often brusque in what she wrote and said, free of substances.

Soon, Jane was gone.

She used to wear a pink breast cancer ribbon on her jacket, Sam wrote. *I haven't looked, but if there's a Crohn's ribbon, you know it's going to be turd brown.*

Fuck Jane, she wrote in a Facebook post. *No, I'd rather fuck Dick, or Spot, because Jane is a pussy.* She edited a picture of the two of them in Provincetown with the words *JANE IS A PUSSY* in bold red lettering, and tagged the picture to Jane's page.

Would you go out with someone who's a*hole was on their abdomen? she wrote to me. *What if she was pretty? What if she gave good head?*

I didn't want to respond to the messages, but I didn't want her to think I was blowing her off, or being "hedgy" towards her, like Jane.

I would if I liked the person, I wrote. Then, afraid that she might take what I'd written wrong, like I was saying *I didn't like her*, I added, in an awkward attempt at humor, *I've gone out with plenty of dudes who clearly had digestive issues.*

She began posting facts about Crohn's Disease on her Facebook page, and joining groups on the site for people with the illness.

Liza messaged me: *I think I'm going to delete Sam. I can't deal with all her posts about her intestinal issues.*

Liza had never had much patience for Sam when she was a client of the halfway house, mostly because of all of her Judy drama, but Sam's posts about her illness were hard to read. She was so forthcoming in her daily indignities, most of which took place in, and around, the bathroom. I'd always thought of myself as a candid person, one who didn't skim on the embarrassing details in the personal essays that I wrote, but Sam's posts were forcing me to acknowledge the hard truth about myself. When it came to bodily functions, especially those involving the digestive tract, I was a big priss. I'd pat myself on the back for my candor in writing about how I'd shot up heroin with water from toilet bowls, but cringed at the idea of anyone imagining me on the toilet.

I could admit to my law-breaking, but not my crap-taking.

The person who had always referenced how "punk rock" she thought I was, had revealed to me my inner Debbie Gibson. If I had an illness like Sam's, would I have had the guts to write about it as candidly as she did?

Sam continued posting her selfies, though in the pictures, she was wearing more clothes: at yoga, because her doctors said exercise was important. At the doctor's office, giving a nurse there a high five. Women were still reaching out to her online, but the relationships seemed to flounder. She was still mostly home-bound. While out on a date, she collapsed in the bathroom of a restaurant, and ended up back in the hospital. She had another operation. There was a likelihood that she would have the colostomy permanently.

I wish I was straight, she messaged me. *At the support groups I've gone to (yes I've been going), the men all hold their wives and g-friend's hands, and talk about trying to make them feel beautiful. I haven't met one woman who can take it. They say it's fine, but get queasy fast.*

On Facebook, she added her "Crohn's stats" to the "About Me" section of her page: her date of diagnosis, her operations, the medications she took.

"She is out and proud about her poop disease now," Liza said.

You are going to love this, Sam wrote to me in a message.

I clicked on the link she sent: it took me to a website with pictures of scantily clad women with colored hair, piercings, tattoos, *and* colostomies. It appeared that she had found the website of the *Suicide Girls* of Irritable Bowel Disease.

I love that they embrace it, she wrote.

Cool, I typed. *Can you put up a profile?*

It's mostly women from Europe. Remember that movie you brought to the halfway house about the car crash people? There are people like that who are turned on by colostomies/stomas.

While Sam and Judy had been on a break, I'd brought some movies to the halfway house for the clients to watch. There was so much down time there on the weekends, I'd often bring in my weird, and sometimes slightly inappropriate, movies from home. One of them had been *Crash.* Based on the J. G. Ballard book of the same name, it was about a subculture of people who were turned on by car accidents. The damage done to the body by an accident became fetishized, a physical reminder of the rush that coincided with the accident.

You don't want to be a fetish, I wrote. *Come on, Sam.*

She was reaching out to me more and more. I felt bad for her, but I also felt burdened. She'd always seemed to romanticize me as someone with stability in their life, though it wasn't true in the way I imagined she thought it was. After I'd become pregnant with my child, I'd reluctantly accepted that I no longer had the luxury of acting like a crazy person.

One weekend while Sam was a client, she'd shown me a dress in her closet that she'd bought with Judy's credit card. I'd been a client of the halfway house, too, a few years before her, and Sam's bedroom had once been my own. While we stood in the closet, I showed her where I'd carved my initials into the wall before I left.

"This is why I love you," she'd said to me then. "No other staff member would ever show a client this. You're clean, but you're still punk rock."

I had turned off the option that indicated to people when I was online because of the number of messages, and photos she'd send to me whenever I logged in.

One morning, she sent me a picture of the red extensions she'd put in her hair. When I saw that she'd sent me a message and another photo a few seconds later, I groaned: I wasn't in the mood.

LOL! she wrote. *Could I make $$? CO-DAZZLE!*

In the picture, she was holding up her shirt, revealing her abdomen. It looked like she had a glittery purse near her hip.

It took a few seconds for it to register: it was her colostomy bag. She'd covered it in stickers, and sparkly decals. She'd *bedazzled* her colostomy bag.

What do you think? she wrote. *Am I punk rock?*

Yes, I typed back. *You're the punkest motherfucker I know.*

She was much more "punk rock" than I was. In the notebook I kept for future writing ideas, I wrote down the title of an essay I hoped to have the guts to write one day.

My Name is Fiona Helmsley. I am a Girl Who Shits.

Then I went into my settings, and turned the "online" option back on.

OF MICE AND MOTHERS

It seemed ironic that *that* mother would be all over the news as the weekend started. That mother. The mother of one of the boys who changed everything. She had just written a book. She had named her son Dylan, after the poet, Dylan Thomas, she tells Diane Sawyer. It is her first public interview since Columbine.

The mother of the ten year old also gave her son a name inspired by a writer. His first name, Emerson. She wasn't a fan of Ralph Waldo Emerson's work so much as she was a fan of a specific quotation attributed to him: The louder he talked of his honor, the faster we counted our spoons. By giving his name to her son, she hoped to always remember it.

Despite having written a book, Dylan's mother says she doesn't identify herself as a writer. Emerson's mother does. She published new writing often, though, according to the tax return she had just filed, it had paid her less than $1,000 the year before. She had told a friend after making the calculation: I might as well have done the writing for free. It almost doesn't seem worth the complications at tax time for an amount so paltry.

Emerson's mom grew up in the town where she was raising him. At the school he attended, they'd shared some of the same teachers. Her and her friends had called in bomb threats for fun back then, in the hopes of getting out of class. The school secretaries would laugh, and hang up the phone. But that was in the early 1990s. In 1999, Dylan and another boy killed 13 people at their high school.

Emerson's mother writes provocative stories. Her more conservative friends had warned her she should be more careful: someday, those stories might be used against you, they said. But it is Emerson, ten years old, who must have a mental health evaluation before he can return to school, because of something he wrote.

Emerson's mother knows the principal, the person saying he must have the evaluation. They went through the school the principal now leads together. While their social circles were always very different, the town was, and remains, small enough that everyone can know the trials and hardships of everyone else. In her day, Emerson's mother had many. She thinks the principal may even remember the bomb threats she and her friends would call in.

Emerson's mother tries to explain to him why he can't go back to school.

He seems confused at first, disbelieving. His next impulse is to deny, because he feels attacked. His mother has a copy of what he wrote, and she shows it to him.

"But what about that book I had to read for class?" he says.

The young male protagonist of the story is thought to be a pussy, until he goes to Vietnam, and proves his courage. Killing was the rite of passage by which a pussy boy proved himself to be a brave man. While Emerson's mother had been surprised by the book, she knew the canon of classic literature was filled with these kinds of stories. But this wasn't Stephen Crane he'd been assigned to read, it was Scholastic. While she'd been surprised that the school was starting kids on these stories so young, she knew she couldn't hide the message of the book from him. It was everywhere. It would always be coming. Instead of complaining, she had read the book with him, and talked with him about it as she helped him transcribe the notes he needed for class.

That morning, at a meeting with the principal, and the school safety officer, Emerson's mother read what her son had written for the first time.

What struck her at first about the highlighted paragraph on the piece of paper was how poorly written it was. She knew it was crass to critique it, but she couldn't help it: she could tell her son hadn't taken the assignment seriously at all. Next, it was the stupidity of it, the emptiness, but to her, that stupidity was tempered by the fact that it had obviously been written by a child. The final thing was how unknowingly he'd pushed all their fear buttons. How innocently he'd walked himself into a world of shit.

Her first instinct was to be cooperative. She started by acknowledging the current environment. The environment post-Dylan, post-Columbine. She acknowledged the school's need to be proactive.

"I see where you might be concerned," she said touching the paper. "But you told me on the phone he wrote this in writing workshop, in a group, with his friends. It's over the top, but it reads to me like something an immature boy would write to make his friends laugh."

"Has he mentioned any thoughts of violence at home?" the school safety officer asked.

"No," Emerson's mother said. "He's never had fake weapons — I don't know what to call them. Toy guns, things like that." Her eyes dropped to the very real gun on the safety officer's belt. "I never allowed them, but it started to seem silly when he could just go to his friends' houses, and play with them. I never objected to video games."

"There's also this," the principal said, pushing a second paper across the table.

On the paper were six words.

Lego Star Wars
Minecraft mod
ISIS

"What is this?" Emerson's mother asked.

"It's a copy of your son's search history from a computer he used in the computer lab a few weeks ago. He searched for ISIS," the safety officer said.

"It's concerning," the principal prompted.

"I'm not trying to make excuses," Emerson's mother said, "But the whole world is talking about ISIS right now. I would imagine classrooms in this school are talking about ISIS. Is this surprising? They're all over the news."

"You let him watch the news?" the principal asked.

You review students' search histories? Emerson's mother thought. "I mean, he doesn't watch the news, but I'll have it on sometimes, and he'll come in the room."

"There was also some concern about his chapter notes for a book. His teacher said his notes focused on the more violent aspects of the story."

"I read that book with him! I did those notes with him!" Emerson's mother said. "Have you read the book? There was nothing else for him to write."

The principal looked at the safety officer.

"If these things were such concerns, Rochelle, why are you only mentioning them to me now?" Emerson's mother said. "He handed in those book notes a month ago. You just said he made this search weeks ago."

"I'm going to ask that you give the safety officer and me a moment alone, so we can talk," the principal said.

As Emerson's mother picked up the papers from the table, she realized she'd called the principal by her first name. This felt like a slip-up. Once her son had started school there, she'd always referred to her by her administrative title. She'd pretended she'd never known her at all.

֍

What Emerson's mother wanted to try to explain to her son would be hard for most ten year-olds to follow. Emerson had always had a harder time understanding the subtle nuances of things more seasoned humans did by default.

Why do I have to be nice to Mr. Kant when he kicks over my bike in the driveway? he'd ask about their landlord. *Why are you so nice* to Aunt Rose when she comes to visit, then say all those mean things about her once she leaves?

It is ok, even encouraged, that you point a fake gun at your friend at a play date.

It is ok, even encouraged, that you tally the number of facsimile kills on a piece of paper at a laser tag birthday party.

It is ok, even required, that you read books with the leitmotif that killing is an act that proves a man's bravery, but you must never betray the influence of these encouragements while you are in school.

This is what Emerson wrote:

> Gary woke up then saw a gun next to him and then he saw a bird so like any baby he shot it and that was his lunch so he thought it was fun killing the eagle so he shot everything in his way a cop and 75 people in all but that toook him 5 years so now he is 6 years old but he still likes to kill people often then out of know where he saw that eagle from 5 years ago so he shot it day one over

Gary was his best friend, one of four boys in a group with him in the writing workshop. One started the story, wrote a paragraph, and passed it on to the next. They had decided their story would be about the adventure of an orphaned baby. They had named the baby after Gary.

After the meeting with the principal, and the school safety officer, Emerson's mother went home. On TV, she watched teaser clips of the Diane Sawyer interview with Dylan's mom.

An hour later, she received a phone call from the principal.

"I am authorizing the safety officer to search your son's locker," she said.

"*Okayyyyy,*" said Emerson's mother, though it wasn't okay. She'd let herself believe that the meeting had been the end of it, that it had been more a critique of her as a parent, than anything having to do with her son.

The next week, in a folder at the psychiatrist's office, she read what was found in her son's locker, from a report written by the safety officer.

Pokémon cards.

An overdue library book about beagles.

A hoodie.

A peanut butter sandwich.

Had the safety officer noticed that the crust had been cut from the sandwich? she wondered. Wasn't that a recognizable illustration of her motherly care?

An hour after the first call, the principal called again.

"I've decided that for the safety of other students, your son should be removed from school until he is psychologically evaluated by a mental health professional," she said.

Emerson's mother threw her purse onto the table, spilling change and the contents of her wallet onto the floor as she hurried to look for her keys.

At the bottom of the safety officer's report, there was a note written in red pen. Emerson's mother could only assume that the safety officer had written it.

Might the eagle be a symbol of the child's disdain for America? I was an English major, it said.

SECONDARY SINS

The second person I ever had sex with was my best friend Maureen's boyfriend, Nate. Since junior high, we'd been a tight threesome, in all ways, except for actual sex. I'd been privy to all the details of their relationship, like how Nate performed cunnilingus on Maureen in a movie theater, and Maureen popped the zits on Nate's back. Nate came up with his own slang for almost everything, and had created jargon for their sex acts. *Touchesit*, he would say, and take Maureen's hand, and put it between his legs. *Fuckesit*, he would say, and depending upon the looks on their faces, I might leave the room.

Nate was good looking, but not very smart. He had a gay uncle who had made it his responsibility that Nate be stylish from a very early age. Nate's hair was dark brown, and every other month, his uncle took him to a salon called Joe Steele to have his bangs bleached blonde. At a time when most of the boys in our grade had no style at all, or one that involved matching hooded bahas with Bugle Boy jeans, Nate looked like a skateboarder slash artist, and wore round, wire-framed glasses with Keith Haring ACT-UP t-shirts. I'd known him since grammar school, where he would put my chair up on top of my desk when I wasn't looking, and blame it on poltergeists. He got into a lot of trouble, both in and outside of school, and had once been taken to the emergency room after being hit by a limo on his skateboard. He'd ridden to the ER draped across the lap of the passenger inside: former Speaker of the House, Tip O'Neill.

Maureen had moved to town in the 6th grade, and made an immediate impression. She was petite and pretty, in a windblown, beachy-wave, California sun- kissed kind of way — Long Beach, California, being where her family had moved from. On the first day of 6th grade, there had been a big commotion in the hallway over a bad smell. When the teachers came out to investigate, Maureen, who no one knew yet, spoke up the loudest: "Someone let out a floating air biscuit!" she said. There were rules to being a new kid; they can be best described by reworking the ancient Greek maxim: *new* kids should be seen and not heard. It never occurred to Maureen to abide by them. By the end of her first week, she was one of the most popular girls in our grade. But it didn't last long.

Maureen and I didn't connect until 7th grade; in 6th grade, her best friend was a girl named Julia. Julia's boyfriend was an 8th grade soccer player named Chris. While Julia was away over a school vacation, Chris came on to Maureen, and told her that his relationship with Julia was over. For some reason, Maureen believed him, and thought this meant it was OK for her and Chris to date. The end of Julia and Chris' relationship turned out to be news to Julia, and soon payphones all over town were covered in red lip-gloss written graffiti: *Maureen L. is a fucking slut! Maureen L.is a fucking tuna!* Maureen broke up with Chris as soon as she found out the truth, but the damage was done. Within a year of moving to town, she was popular girl non-grata. It was during this time that she had gotten together with Nate. He wasn't just her boyfriend, he was her only friend. The two of them seemed to exist in their own private world.

The scandal surrounding Maureen made her intriguing to me. She'd ascended to such impressive social heights, only to plummet. I heard Julia make threats of violence against her. She was going to kick Maureen's ass — she was going *to kick her ass through adolescence*. So what if Chris had lied to Maureen? *It took two to tango.* I envisioned Chris beckoning Maureen to a sexy dance with a crooked finger. I imagined Julia's foot planted so firmly in Maureen's behind that it aged her until she looked like a high school senior.

The beating that would speed Maureen's adult development was to occur the night of the Torchlight parade, our small town's annual winter holiday celebration. As the high school band played *Jingle Bell Rock* and the Boy Scouts handed out hot chocolate, Maureen was attacked, not by Julia, but by Julia's new best friend, Leanna. It was pure opportunism on Leanna's part: she'd had a sexual encounter with Nate before he had gotten together with Maureen, and he'd described her private parts to anyone willing to listen as being like "Jell-O and sandpaper." Nate had also come up with the nickname for Leanna that people used behind her back: *Green Teeth*. Leanna's teeth had an unfortunate, dingy tinge to them. Leanna attacked Maureen to impress Julia, but also to get back at Nate, by proxy.

Maureen's reaction to the parade assault made her even more intriguing to me. Yes, technically, Green Teeth had kicked her ass. She'd thrown Maureen into the bushes along the parade route, and ripped her pants. But what difference had it made? If Julia and Leanna hoped to humiliate Maureen, it didn't work. She hadn't tried to hide that night, or run away. The next week at school, she even wore the ripped pants. Maureen refused to be intimidated. I wondered what it would be like to be her friend.

Every day at lunch in 7th grade, we had two choices about where to eat: the cafeteria, which was across campus, or the Estuary Council. The Estuary Council was an organization run out of the school that offered meals and low-impact activities to the local elderly. The Estuary Council was closer, but eating there meant you had to share your lunch table with old people. Nate and Maureen always ate at the Estuary Council. I remember knowing as I put my tray down next to them, and a septuagenarian in a bow tie, that battle lines were being drawn. I knew that some of my friends would no longer talk to me, and would consider me to be a traitor. By junior high standards I was making a bold move, but I wanted to be bold.

The quickest way to cement a close friendship is to assume the other person's problems, and Maureen's problems became my own. We immediately went about planning how to get revenge on Green Teeth. I had insight into Leanna that Maureen didn't, as Leanna and I had once been good friends. I knew how horrified she'd been by Nate's description of her private parts, and while I was at my grandmother's house, came across something that I thought we could use in her mail: a free sample of the vaginal cream, Vagisil.

I wasn't one hundred percent sure what Vagisil was used for, but recognized it as a shame-inducing feminine product — the kind of product you were supposed to hide in your shopping basket, if you were to buy it at the drugstore. Nate liked the sound of the word "Vagisil" and added it to his lexicon of invented slang, which also included pop culture references: *Freedom Rock. Suckesit. Vagisil.* The next day, Maureen and I put the Vagisil in Green Teeth's locker.

Green Teeth's vengeance was quick and vicious. She confronted Maureen while she was alone in the bathroom, and punched her hard in the stomach. Maureen was in so much pain afterward, she was taken from the school, in an ambulance. She found out from her hospital bed that the pain she felt wasn't damage done by Green Teeth, but was due to having cysts on her ovaries. Despite her doctor's claims otherwise, we assumed the cysts had formed because she and Nate had started having sex, and she was so tiny.

It was while Maureen was out of commission with the cysts that rumors first started that Nate had cheated on her. Even if Maureen had taken those early rumors seriously, ending their relationship would have been hard. Over the period when she had no friends but him, their lives had become totally intertwined, *enmeshed*. Nate would go on vacations with her family, and spend whole weekends at her house, sleeping in her room. Maureen was close with Nate's mom and siblings, who treated her like a surrogate daughter, or teenaged sister-in-law. Breaking up would have meant the end of all of those relationships — and that those people would have *opinions* on ending the relationship, too. And Nate would deny, deny, deny, swearing on seemingly sacred things, like his mom, and the Bible. Eventually, there were so many rumors that Maureen had to take them seriously, and by the summer going into our freshman year of high school, Nate and Maureen fell into a pattern of breaking up and making up, breaking up and making up.

I entered high school with two goals: to try LSD and to "try" sex. That was the way I thought about sex before I had it — abstractly, as something to experience. Looking back, I think there were times while I was young that my curiosity acted as a corrupting agent. It led me to view meaning as an obstacle, something that got in the way. Or maybe it was just fear. Perhaps I had already figured out that to invest something with meaning was to it give it the power to hurt you.

My freshman year, Maureen and Nate were the only people I knew having sex. Although Nate enjoyed talking about the intricacies of their sex life in front of me, it wasn't something I could vicariously experience through them. I had started going out with a boy who was also a virgin, but he was shy. Sex was a big deal to him — not something to be done just for "the experience." Though I cared about him, I found it hard to wait, and even harder to broach the subject with him. Among my new friends was a loud, obnoxious boy, a drummer in a local cover band. He was a notorious horndog with a conquest list a mile long. One night I snuck out of my house to meet him, knowing what would happen. The loud, obnoxious boy and notorious horndog was one of my boyfriend's best friends.

I told Nate and Maureen what I had done. They seemed to understand what I had been after: *the experience.* Though they liked my boyfriend, I knew they could be trusted to keep it a secret.

And they had their own problems. By this point, Maureen and Nate were breaking up and making up constantly. One night, Maureen couldn't find Nate, and we heard that he had spent the night at another girl's house, a few towns away. We found out where the girl lived, and stormed her house, finding a bedheaded Nate at her kitchen table, eating breakfast. Maureen shoved his head into the bowl of cereal in front of him, as the girl's mother called the cops. Not long after, my boyfriend found out what I had done. He refused to hear my ridiculous explanation. He wrote me a scathing letter calling me both a whore and a prude. He wrote that I'd put out for anyone — as long as they weren't him.

Feeling beaten down by the men in our lives, Maureen and I decided to run away. A friend's grandmother had just died, and she'd given me boxes of her unsold Avon jewelry. Maureen and I planned to hitchhike to California, and sell the jewelry at Grateful Dead shows, only we never made it out of town. Our parents found our goodbye notes, and tracked us to a friend's house. Nate used Maureen's parents concern for her to weasel his way back into her life.

Maybe Nate was smarter than I'm willing to admit. Without him in her life, Maureen really had no one else but me. Though her social standing had improved since junior high, in the minds of many of our classmates, especially the female ones, she'd been defined by the Julia/Chris debacle: she was a "boyfriend stealer," someone who couldn't be trusted. It didn't matter that in the years since she'd been in a committed relationship, while her boyfriend cheated on her. Maureen didn't try to change anyone's opinion. She had me, and she had Nate. In spite of his betrayals, she must have thought this was enough. Though Nate was my friend, too, whenever I was dragged into their relationship, I always sided with Maureen.

Besides spending the night at their house, in Maureen's room, and joining them on their family vacations, Maureen's parents let Nate drive their car once he got his license. They let Nate and me be in their house when they weren't there — and when Maureen wasn't there, either. This was the case, one day, when Maureen was sick. Her mom took her to a doctor's appointment, and Nate and I stayed behind at the house.

There was a crumpled sleeping bag on the floor of Maureen's room. As Nate explained to me, once we were alone, he'd spent the night, playing Florence Nightingale to the ill Maureen. He had selflessly slept on the floor to avoid getting sick himself.

He straightened out the sleeping bag, then laid down on top of it.

"It's so cozy!" he said, nuzzling into it exaggeratedly. "I couldn't sleep last night with Maureen's coughing. Lie down with me. Let's take a nap." He reached up to grab my arms. We'd been friends for so long, and had innocently played around before. He pulled me on to the floor next to him, then started flopping around on top of the sleeping bag, as if he couldn't get comfortable.

Nate smelled good. It was another thing his uncle had impressed upon him early — wearing cologne. It was a light, clean smell, always on the t-shirts of his that I would find lying around Maureen's room.

"I can't sleep," he said, looking down in an exaggerated way that directed my eyes to the bulge in his Army shorts. *"Fuckesit?"*

"Nate!" I said. Though his cheating was common knowledge, it was still shocking to hear him blatantly admit to it, and to admit to it by asking me to cheat with him.

"Come on," he said. *"Fuckesit.* You know if you and Maureen weren't good friends, you and I would have a long time ago."

I didn't know this. Nate had been Maureen's boyfriend for so many years that I had come to see him as an extension of her. Before Maureen, I'd recognized Nate as being attractive, probably the best looking boy in our grade, but had interpreted this to mean he was too good looking to ever be interested in me. Though the veracity of his statement was in question — *you and I would have a long time ago* — it still felt flattering. *Nate wants to fuck me.* I guess it didn't take much.

"Yes," he said, unbuttoning his shorts. "You must help me. *Fuckesit.*"

He pulled his shorts down to his knees, revealing his plaid boxers. His hard penis poked out through the opening. I think, even then, I recognized that I was looking at a weapon. He gave me a coy look, both mischievous and playful, a slightly different version of a look I'd seen him give Maureen many times. He believed in his charm one hundred percent. The look said *I want to do a bad thing. I believe I can get away with it. Do it with me.* I didn't disagree with the look. He reached over and unbuttoned my pants.

As Nate fucked me, I thought to myself, *I guess I'm a shitbag, too.* I moved my mouth towards his to kiss him, not out of any need, or strong desire, but because I thought that was what you did when you had sex. He hesitated for a moment, then kissed me in a way that felt mechanical. In spite of this, physically, sex with my best friend's boyfriend was better than sex with one of my boyfriend's best friends. Nate was good at it. I figured it was because of his years of experience with Maureen.

After Maureen got back from the doctor, and Nate left in her father's car to pick up her prescriptions, she gave me a slightly *different* version of the night before. She said that Nate wouldn't stop pawing at her. She'd told him again and again how sick she felt, and finally, dejectedly, and with a little pout on his face, he had gotten the sleeping bag out of the closet and moved to the floor.

I wondered to myself — does he need sex so badly that if Maureen's sick for a night, he has to go and find it somewhere else? Hadn't his cheating started back in junior high, when Maureen had been laid up with the cysts? Only this time I couldn't tell Maureen my new theory, because I was complicit. It was a dumb theory anyway, one that explained nothing, because Nate didn't just cheat on Maureen when she was sick — he cheated on her all the time, whenever he could. When Nate brought me home later in her father's car, we made a detour to a cul de sac at the end of street. We had sex again, on the hood of the car. I could see Maureen's house from where we parked. The light was on in her bedroom.

Sex with Nate, though physically satisfying, had heavy and immediate emotional repercussions. The secret became like a fourth person in our relationship. As Maureen and Nate continued to argue over his cheating, I could do nothing but sit there, like a lump. I now knew for certain the lengths Nate would go to lie. A purse was found in his new car, with the ID of a girl we went to school with inside it. I was sure the girl had left it there on purpose, hoping that Maureen would find it. Without asking me, Nate claimed I had found the bag, and gave it to him to return. The secret pacified me as Maureen's loyal ally. I didn't know what to say anymore, now that I was a part of the lie.

Finally, our sophomore year, Maureen started to see someone else. She was finally ready to strike out on her own, without Nate. This was big: for the longest time I couldn't even get her to admit that she found other men attractive, not even celebrities. There had been a time when Nate wouldn't admit to finding any other women attractive, either. They talked about, and agreed: they would each be allowed one celebrity crush. Maureen chose Richard Grieco. Nate chose Mariah Carey. But those first love courtesies, back in 7th grade, seemed so long ago.

Nate must have felt deeply threatened. Later, when I asked him why he did what he had done, he couldn't give me an answer. He once again tried to fall back on being cute, and made a face. Why did I? Selfishness? Immaturity? Low self-esteem? I had always believed my conscience would act as a barrier, a final fortification, until it didn't.

Though Maureen was seeing someone, a boy from another town who she'd met at a party, Nate, was, of course, still in her life. They were no longer together, but their lives were still intertwined. She had to see him at school, where they shared classes, where he'd wait for her outside her classroom, in the hallway, to start a fight, or to claim that he still had something important that he needed at her house. Sometimes, he'd stalk past her with a girl on his arm. He must have felt that these deliberate acts were no longer eliciting much of a response.

Maureen and I were in French class when Nate appeared outside the door of the classroom. A few weeks before, Maureen might have asked to get a drink from the water fountain so she could go out, and give him a kiss. This time, she ignored him. He turned his attention to me, and gestured that I come out.

I turned to Maureen.

"Should I see what he wants?" I asked.

She rolled her eyes. "I guess."

I asked to go to the bathroom, and joined Nate in the hallway.

"This has to stop," I said. I could have meant us, but I meant his harassment of Maureen.

"I know," Nate said with a dopey grin. There was no one else in the hallway, and he grabbed my hand.

"*Touchesit?*" he said.

"Stop it," I said. "What do you want?"

In his hand, he had a folded up piece of paper.

"Give this to Maureen," he said.

"Come on," I said. "You need to leave her alone. You both need to move on."

"I know, I know," he said. "I am. I promise."

I started to open it.

"No," he said. "Don't open it. Just give it to her. It'll be funny, I swear. I'm going to stand in the hallway, and watch."

"It better not be anything hurtful," I said, knowing better.

I went back to the classroom, and when the teacher wasn't looking, passed the note to Maureen.

"He wants me to give this to you," I said.

Once again, she rolled her eyes. For a few seconds, my attention went to the teacher.

When I turned back around, Maureen was getting up. I never saw her face. I looked towards the door, and saw Nate standing there. She rushed past him, then out of view.

I looked back at her desk, and saw the note there, unfolded.

It said:

ASK YOUR BEST FRIEND WHAT SHE DID WITH ME

I looked up towards the door, and my eyes met Nate's.

He was still making that dopey face.

Then he was gone, too.

THE RAPE BOOK

Pat Hackett wrote that one of the harder things about editing Andy Warhol's diaries for publication was his use of hyperbole and exaggeration. Eighteen was a number he used like a loose plural; in Warhol's daily accounts, it could mean any amount greater than one. His physical descriptions of people didn't always line up with their reality: if someone was short, he made them shorter. If they were fat, he made them even more rotund.

It's April, and my old friend Marie is coming to the area to visit her family. From the ages of ten to sixteen, we were close friends. When I'm thinking of writing about something from that time in our lives, I'll sometimes contact her, and ask her what she remembers. She's begun to act burdened by my inquiries. She finds much of what I ask her about embarrassing. I'm starting to think she wants to believe that she came into the world fully formed, that she never drank 'til she puked, or made out with a girl just to impress a guy.

"Hey," she says when I call her. "Do you want to try to meet up while I'm there?"

"Sure," I say. "But I'm starting to write a story, and wanted to ask you some pesky questions."

"My motivations for being Team Feldman over Team Haim?"

"No. I wanted to ask you about The Rape Book."

"The what?"

"The Rape Book. The notebook we started with the list of boy's names, boys that we wanted to rape us. That's what we called it. We must have been about eleven."

"I have no idea what you are talking about."

"You don't remember? I still have it."

"If I wrote down the names of boys who I wanted to rape me, I meant it facetiously. What I meant was, I thought they were cute. Nobody wants to be raped."

"Do you want me to read to you some of the names of the boys that you wrote?"

"You probably wrote them."

"We both did."

"It's probably just a list of boys that I thought were cute."

"You don't think it's strange we used the word "rape"?"

"No. I think it's exaggeration. Immature humor. What's the word...hyperbole. "

℘

There is a scene in the Andy Warhol (produced, Paul Morrissey written and directed) film *Trash* where the hapless, heroin-addicted Joe Dallesandro breaks into the apartment of the giddily- happy-to- be- victimized Jane Forth. Catching him in her living room, Jane asks, her voice tinged with leading anticipation, "Are you a rapist?" Joe, intuiting what the right answer is, says, "Yeah, yeah," but not very convincingly.

My first sexual fantasy involved being raped by Micky Dolenz, drummer of the 1960s made for television rock group The Monkees. I watched the TV show religiously, in re-runs, from the ages of about nine to twelve. I was the kind of devoted fan wherein if you didn't like the Monkees, I thought less of you. (In The Rape Book, a male classmate is listed as a desirable rapist, but next to his name is a mark —a demerit—because he doesn't like The Monkees.) The fantasy was a nightly projection that I indulged in at bedtime, and always like this, with some slight variations, like the color and style of my bathing suit, or what real-life friends I bestowed the imaginary honor of hanging out with the group with me:

We are at the beach. We play volleyball, boys (The Monkees) against girls (my real-life friends). There is a lot of flirting, playful rough- housing, and kicking of sand. (It's interesting to think about the amount of "playful" violence involved in juvenile flirting. It's often through "playful" violence that we first give ourselves permission to reach out, and touch.) Micky and I slip off to the dunes, where we frolic for a bit, like something from a Doris Day film, or a Monkees episode where the boys have love interests. There, away from the others, Micky overpowers me. After a brief, yet physically accurate struggle, he tears off my swimsuit, and rapes me in the sand.

Afterward, he and I walk back to my friends and the rest of the group holding hands. Micky Dolenz has raped me, and I'm glowing. My swimsuit, which I look great in, and has magically melted away all my baby fat, has also regenerated itself.

ళ

Marie is right; there is no such thing as a "rape fantasy." The two words side by side are in contradiction. In my Micky Dolenz "rape fantasy" nothing *truly* forced or unwanted happened; the violence was just posturing. But these postures of violence were absolutely necessary, my whole fantasy hinged upon them. I needed the violence there in order to give myself permission to fantasize about sex.

On the phone, Marie says, her voice devoid of any remaining vestiges of patience, "So, what, you think that you meant it? You think that you really wanted to be raped?"

Because it would be too easy for me to say *no* (I don't like the way she's talking to me, and it would make me feel like I was making a concession to her), and too involved for me to say, "I think I wanted to give myself permission," I start to say something pretentious, about the "etymology" of word choices, but she cuts me off.

"It bothers me when I think about the way I just followed you. You were always the idea person. Your obsession with The Monkees? When we were ten, they were our parent's ages. And later, your fascination with all those deviant art people? Andy Warhol? I can't help you with this. I was just a spectator. Your captive audience of one."

We don't meet up when she visits.

℘

I see a therapist, and tell her I am attempting to write an essay about the origins of rape fantasies.

She says, *Brava. It's sure to be a narrative with elements of guilt, shame, lust, gender disparity.*

Lazy language, too, I say.

She asks if I write under a pen name.

I never really thought of it as a pen name, I say. *It started as a "punk name," a name I used to answer personal ads in the back of MaximiumRockNRoll. But since I'm about to have a birthday that makes me officially middle-aged, and I still use it, maybe I should start referring to it as one.*

Yes, I say, practicing. *I write under a pen name.*

Good, she says.

℘

Brigid Berlin, *Brigid Polk, Brigid Pork*, is my favorite Warhol superstar. Now in her late 70s, Brigid has always been open about her tortured relationship with food. The documentary about her life, *Pie in the Sky*, takes its name from all the key lime pie she'd like to eat one day, guilt-free. The physical results of Brigid's compulsion to stuff her mouth — her fatness — never shut her mouth. To be fat and unabashed when you are a woman is an act of rebellion.

In a scene from the David Weisman film *Ciao Manhattan*, Brigid sits on what appears to be a toilet in a bathroom stall, wearing a small bikini top. She talks to the camera about all the expensive châteauxs and camps she's been sent to by her family to lose weight. She stands up, and defiantly jabs a syringe of methamphetamine into her large, shapely ass. Brigid's mother first started her on speed as a child to help curb her appetite: what her mother had hoped would reduce her, instead emboldened her. Speed helped to fuel her art — prints she made with her often exposed tits, and inspired some of her most memorable cinematic diatribes. On speed, Brigid became larger and *louder*, the opposite of her mother's intentions.

I love loud women, and in Brigid Berlin I see a specific type of loud woman, a woman, who, despite the constant physical rejection she experienced, didn't go inward, didn't go *quiet*, but instead, made herself more visible. The default message to all women deemed undesirable by society is *if you insist on continuing in your unfuckable state of existence, kindly do it quietly*. Being loud after registering continuous opposition to your presence is *some nerve*. My favorite loud women are always like Brigid: smart, funny, aggressively unpredictable. "Unsightly" women who aren't afraid to make scenes.

For a period, in my teens, I was one. Being loud was a quality that helped me to root out the good men from the bad. The bad men had no use for me because I wasn't attractive, and my loudness made me even more unappealing (I was spat on by a boy, when I was thirteen, for being ugly and loud), but the good men whose interests I couldn't foster with my looks, I drew to me by being smart, and funny, qualities I communicated to them via my loudness — in essence, *obfuscating my looks*. It was during this time that I had my first real boyfriend. He was an intellectual; however intellectual one can be at seventeen. He was sensitive, two years older, and maybe a tad gay. When we got together, I was a virgin, a virgin fixated on the idea of having sex. He was also a virgin, but we never talked about it. We'd fool around in the backseat of his mother's car, and despite my loudness, my social boldness, I'd feel paralyzed to touch him back. Because he was a good man, he didn't force the issue. My interest in sex got stronger, but I always felt too ashamed to broach the subject with him. So at fifteen, I did what stereotyped men in oppressive cultures do when they fear soiling their beloveds. Behind his back, I sought out the services of one of the most promiscuous boys at school, and had sex with him.

As I became more attractive, I stopped being so loud. Social boldness doesn't come as naturally to me anymore. Some might say that's maturity, but I disagree. I think I lost something once I became more attractive to men, some kind of fighting spirit. By being told again and again that I was ugly when I was young, I developed guts, out of necessity. I wanted too desperately to be acknowledged, to feel that I was being seen.

But "guts" and confidence aren't the same thing. "Guts" are more impulsive, and situational. Confidence is a belief.

Though I was loud in speaking my mind — except when it came to matters of wanting sex — what I wanted was to be physically desired by men without having to speak up, and advocate for myself, first. What I wanted most as a young girl was to be physically desired by less than good men.

I had this idea that physical desirability was some kind of irresistible urge. Men on the street, their cat calls: you were desirable when men couldn't control their need to tell you that you were. There was a point, after I became more attractive to men, when, if they didn't call out to me on the street in some sexually suggestive way, I'd feel bad about myself, less than. There were times I'd go out at night just for the reaffirmation of their voices: their nasty words. I'd go out at night looking for strangers to call out in my direction that they wanted to fuck me.

While I was living in New York City, my landlady noticed, and became concerned. She'd see me leaving my apartment, late at night, alone. "If you insist on going out now, all by yourself," she'd say, never realizing she was reaffirming my juvenile beliefs, "At least make yourself ugly first."

"I just do art because I'm ugly and there is nothing else for me to do," Andy Warhol said.

❧

It would be too pat to call me a narcissist. I've held onto boxes of personal artifacts, and spent some time with the luxury that comes from being removed from events, trying to make sense of them.

While I fantasized about rape, I wrote about guilt.

Spelling intact — journal entries, eleven years old:

> *Tuesday, Dec. 8, 1987*
> *I'm feeling very sexy today. My hair looks irrestiable. I have on scimpy underwear, and no top. If a cute guy where here, the bed would be thumpin. I hope mom never finds this. I better find a better finding spot.*

> *Fri. Dec. 11, 1987*
> *I'm watching "Sixteen Candles." Mrs. Clark and I gott into a huge fight. Just because I wouldn't babysit tonight. That entry that I wrote before this is DISGUSTING AND GROSS. I don't know what I was thinking.*

❧

A pivotal memory from my childhood is the time that I thought I was pregnant by the family dog. A few years ago, I wrote a short story about it, making it all very funny, ha ha hee hee, and while the idea of being that naive is funny, the reality was traumatizing. It is one of my clearest childhood memories.

I didn't understand reproduction, let alone the impossibility of inter-species reproduction, but I knew that penises played a role in the making of babies, and because our dog had rubbed his penis on my leg, deduced this to mean I'd be having a baby of my own. Human, or canine, I don't know. I assume I thought it would be human. The point is what I did because I thought I was pregnant.

I stood at the top of the stairs to our basement, and tried to throw myself down. It was a steep decline, and I couldn't do it, so I punched myself in the stomach again and again. I felt intense, frightening shame. I was afraid of what would happen once everyone found out. I thought my family would disown me. I thought my life was over.

I was eight.

In the essay that I wrote, making it all very funny, the resolution comes at night while I'm saying prayers with my mother. We are Catholics, and while praying to the Virgin Mary, I ask my mother what "virgin" means. She gives me a G-rated answer, and then I ask her if it was possible that Jesus' father was a dog. After getting huffy at the sacrilege, she tells me that humans cannot make babies with animals.

I don't remember how I learned I was not pregnant by the family dog. In 1984, when I was eight, there was no internet I could just type an anonymous search query into. Maybe I asked my older sister, in some coy way. However I learned, I was intensely relieved.

Seven years later, at fifteen, I had my first real pregnancy scare, after another encounter with the promiscuous boy. I did the same thing I did when I was eight. I punched myself in the stomach. We'd moved to a different house, where I successfully threw myself down the stairs. I wasn't pregnant.

In the late 1990s, there was a rash of highly-publicized incidents of young women giving birth alone: no one had known the young women were pregnant. The babies died, and it became a legal matter (and media sideshow) to determine how: had the babies been born dead, or had the young women acted in some way to deliberately end their lives. The women were called monsters and cold-blooded murderers. At the same time, they were parodied and laughed at. They became media spectacles.

I felt a kinship with those young women; if not for circumstance, their actions might have been my own. After giving birth, one of the women had made a primitive attempt to clean herself up, then joined her friends on the dance floor. She had given birth in the bathroom during her high school prom.

The women all did jail time, then disappeared into quiet, anonymous lives. How else to explain the near-zero recidivism rates for these "monsters, cold-blooded murderers," besides you're only a young woman once?

&

Arguably, Andy Warhol's best-known cinematic contributions are his 2-4 minute "film portraits" now known as *The Screen Tests*. Modeled after the classic Hollywood audition process, Warhol's screen tests are a virtual trading card series of 1960s downtown cool. Diane Di Prima, Susan Sontag, Amy Taubin, and Yoko Ono all sat (with varying degrees of patience) for Warhol's camera. Though many of the screen tests were not saved, close to 500 people sat for the series between 1964 and 1967.

Underground actress Mary Woronov said, "...I think for Warhol, the screen test was *not* that. I believe Warhol was afraid of people. For a guy who is afraid of people, to finally have this person sitting in front of him, looking at him! But it wasn't the person; it was the film of the person, and he would become close, whereas with real people he couldn't achieve that. So he was actually sexually fantasying, sexually fascinated, and that is why the screen tests kept on happening."

ᥱ᥍

Recently, I started watching the first season of *Mork and Mindy*, a comedy sitcom I watched often as a kid. The show originally ran from the late 1970s to the early 1980s, before it was cancelled in 1982, when I was six. I watched it mostly in re-runs.

In the premiere episode, Mork, a human-looking alien from the planet Orc, meets Mindy, a twenty-one year old woman employed at her father's music store, when his space egg lands in the park where she is being sexually accosted by her new boyfriend.

"It only took you three days to attack me like a Thanksgiving turkey!" Mindy says, as they struggle. "I like it when you talk dirty!" her boyfriend replies. After a final, angry exchange, her boyfriend takes off in her car, leaving Mindy in the park all alone, at night.

Most of the TV programming considered to be family- friendly during my formative years showed sex like this: for young women, it appeared to be a continuous battle of near misses and close calls. The man pushed, sex! The woman pushed back, *no sex*! The man squeezed, *sex*! Still, she managed to wiggle free, *no sex*! Sometimes, outside male intervention was required, and this was viewed as heroic; often she fell in love with this man afterward, as a reward. *He saved her, so he got her.*

Watching at home, it could be very confusing. If the woman always resisted, yet the man continued to push, then desirability had to be some kind of irresistible urge, right? The man had to be powerless to control himself. To a young person, one who still believed in the inherent goodness of most everyone, this could seem like a logical conclusion. It kept the man blameless, and free of actual evil intent. It also put forth the idea that there was something covetable to this kind of male response. Pam Dawber, the actress who played Mindy, had been a popular model; in Warhol parlance, she was a member of what he viewed as a venerable social caste, an exclusive group he termed "beauties." To watch her character be treated like this by men, and not just Mindy, but most of the female characters held up as "beauties" on television, was to be inoculated with the idea that this was *how* men responded to beautiful women. This kind of reaction became the proof, and a salve to warding off physical insecurity—perhaps a woman's real desirability, her true attractiveness, could be measured by the animal response of the men around her.

Mindy notices Mork in the park after the encounter with her boyfriend, and she assumes he is a priest because it's dark, and he has his suit on backwards. She confides in him what's just happened with her boyfriend, because she thinks she can trust him as a man of God. Continuing to act on this assumption, she brings Mork back to her house, and in the light of her living room, sees that Mork's clothes are backwards, and he is not a priest. She starts to scream, and backs away from Mork in terror. Mork, the supposedly naïf alien asks her, "Is screaming your way of saying thanks?"

In the first half of the show, Mindy has faced sexual assault, feared sexual assault, and managed to avoid it, twice. But she's not out of the woods yet.

At the door, a space egg arrives. It carries Mork's lost interplanetary luggage. The arrival of the space egg finally convinces Mindy that Mork is as he says, an alien, and not an attacker. Sprawled defensively, yet adorably across a chair in her living room, she asks him once more, to be sure, "You're not going to hurt me, are you?"

Mork explains to Mindy he's been sent to Earth to observe and gather data on mankind, and she agrees to let him stay with her, at her house, platonically, for the time being. When Mindy's father finds out she has a man staying with her, he treats it as a personal betrayal. He goes to his liquor cabinet, and gets drunk on the wine he's been saving for years for Mindy's wedding, because now that she's let a man spend the night at her house, as far as he's concerned, there will never be any wedding for Mindy.

He cries out to his friends as he drinks, "My daughter is a loose woman… I don't know how to tighten her!"

༼

In most of the television I watched, the consequences to young women who were *receptive* to a man's advances were hardly ever pregnancy (praise the pill?). They were shame, slander, and self-loathing. (The self-loathing often took the form of emotional regret for parting with her virginity too soon, or not under "ideal" circumstances.) But when the woman rejected, or successfully thwarted, the man's advances, there were *still* shame-related consequences for her to contend with — and the man could always lie to assuage his bruised ego.

Sex was shown as something that was taken from young women, or used against them. Often, it was both. Going by what I saw on TV, the best a young woman might hope for when it came to sex was that whatever happened — and this was clear, sex was something that *happened* to women — happened quickly, and quietly. This may be why it seemed like so many female characters in the media I watched, and the books I read, said things like, "I'd rather be killed than raped." The after-effects of rape, as well as consensual sex, could go on and on. Death, at least, was final.

This may be what Pa Ingalls, I mean Michael Landon, thought — it was better for a young woman to die afterward than live. It was Landon who wrote and directed the two-part *Little House on the Prairie* episode entitled "Sylvia." The storyline was considered compelling enough that it first aired in 1981, during network sweeps week.

ॐ

Little House on the Prairie may have been historical fiction, but it dealt with contemporary issues: that was part of the show's appeal. The car may have replaced the horse and buggy, and the superstore the general store, but the human condition transcends time.

The "Sylvia" storyline shares some of the same plot points as Stephen King's *Carrie*, but the sweet and kind-hearted girl at its center never gets her revenge. Instead of a religiously- wacko mother, 15 year old Sylvia Webb has a bitter, domineering father, who is further put upon by the fact that she, his only child, is going through puberty. When Albert Ingalls and his friends are caught trying to leer into Sylvia's bedroom windows, Sylvia's father blames Sylvia. He makes her bind her breasts, as he comments about her deceased mother's supposedly promiscuous behavior. Albert feels bad for his part in the leering, and elects to get to know Sylvia *as a person*. (To this end, Albert punches a friend of his in the face, because of the suggestive comments the friend continues to make about Sylvia.) Albert realizes that he's romantically interested in Sylvia, and they embark on a relationship in secret. But her father finds out and forbids Sylvia to see Albert. Though it's not what she wants, the dutiful Sylvia complies. One day, while walking through the woods, she stops to pick flowers. A man in a creepy Kabuki mask wraps his gloved hand over her mouth, and drags her into the woods. Later that night, Sylvia crawls home. "You reap what you sow," her father says. He puts the beaten and bruised girl into bed, and forbids her to tell anyone what's happened.

Throughout the two-part episode, Sylvia is treated like an object, a *thing* whose purpose is to be debated and parsed by others, primarily men. Desiring her, the boys of Walnut Grove peep at her. Because she's started to develop breasts, her father — and Mrs. Oleson, who calls a *town meeting* — decide she's a wanton seductress. Albert, in an act that's supposed to be seen as redemptive, in light of his participation in the leering, decides she's a girl he'd like to romance, and later, adding to his heroic arc, marry. Knowing her father won't allow the relationship, Sylvia makes her one and only decision of the two episodes: to briefly defy her father, and date Albert. It's while she's staying away from Albert, as she's been told instructed by her father, that she is attacked, and dragged into the woods.

At the end of "Sylvia" part 1, we learn she's pregnant by her attacker, though the word "rape" is never used. In part 2, after initially reacting with rage at the betrayal he imagines must be inherent to her pregnancy, Albert decides he wants to marry Sylvia, and offers her, and the child she will be having, the veneer of legitimacy. They run away, and stop at a barn, where Albert leaves Sylvia to wait while he goes to gather money for their trip. While she is alone there, Sylvia's rapist returns. As she tries to escape from him, she is injured. Her father, who has been out searching for Sylvia, discovers her at the barn, and shoots her rapist. But there is no happy ending. Sylvia dies from her injuries.

Everything that occurs over the course of the storyline is supposed to be connected to Sylvia's burgeoning sexuality, but this idea is not only offensive; visually, it's hard to comprehend. We are told again and again that Sylvia has "matured faster" than the other girls in Walnut Grove, but the actress who plays Sylvia looks like all the other young girls in the episode: totally adolescent. It's as if a concise *TV Guide*-type synopsis of the "Sylvia" storyline might be this: *the men of Walnut Grove react in panic to the threat of a young girl's training bra.*

"Sylvia" as a story is miserable, but as a young girl, I was still able to see something in it that I wanted. Sylvia's desirability was the focus, and she was so desirable, she was able to snag the interest of Albert Ingalls. (I thought Albert was so cute.) I saw this as power.

When we venerate physical beauty as adults, most often, what we are really venerating is the power that we imagine we would get from that beauty, and how we would use that power to change our lives. As a young girl, I saw the desire of men as the end all/be all. I saw the desire of men as the power itself. I saw power in being chosen, *crowned*, by men as an object, a *thing*.

Though I didn't fully understand what had happened to Sylvia in the woods the first few times I watched the episode, the way her rape remained unspoken, yet recognizable at the same time as something tawdry, resonated with me. It was the way I was coming to identify sex, to recognize the subject of it, at home. By what wasn't being said. By what was deliberately left out. By the tone of a voice, or a look.

This made every sly mention, every low-key reference I was able to pick up on—thrilling. The thrill didn't discriminate. It could be a raunchy joke, or a passage in book about a "throbbing manhood." It could be an act that involved violence, or one that was described as "love-making." As a young girl, I didn't see much distinction. What did it matter? It was all shameful.

I believe this lack of distinction contributed to my fantasies.

✑

In 1965, Andy Warhol facilitated the production of the film *Beauty #2*.

In the film, a scantily-clad Edie Sedgwick shares a room with two men. One man is seen: the handsome Gino Perschio, who Edie lounges on a large bed with. The other man sits somewhere off-screen. His name is Chuck Wein. Wein met Edie at their mutual therapist's office. After a few years of close friendship, he took on the role of her manager. Wein travelled from Massachusetts to New York City with Edie, ostensibly to help launch her career as an actress, and a model.

As Edie lounges on the bed with Gino, the unseen Chuck plies her with questions. The questions are conversational at first, light, if a bit superficial. He asks her about her earrings, and her fashion sense. He mentions pets he knows she had growing up. Then his tone changes. He critiques the believability of her sexual interest in Gino, who, at Chuck's direction, Edie kisses, and rolls around with on the bed. "You can do better than that, Edie," Wein says. "He's not even hard." He references her father's sexual abuse: "If you were only older Gino, you could be her daddy." He mentions her drug issues: "I hope the next 35 minutes are fun, then you can get tired, and I can give you your pills... I'll wake you up tomorrow, we'll find another doctor."

Warhol often encouraged the provocation of actors in his films, but it wasWein who came up with the concept of this unscripted movie for Edie, using personal things she had confided in him as fodder.

"Why don't you just give up?" Wein says. "You can't feel anything."

Film critic Amy Taubin said, "The story of Beauty #2 is a story of a woman being pulled apart, invaded from three different directions. That's a common situation for women, it happens in reality, and it happens in fantasy. Here you have the camera staring at her from one angle, there's this guy, Chuck Wein, baiting her from another side and there's this guy sitting on her bed and he's trying to get her to pay attention to him... And she's in the midst of this posed in a fashion model type of way to show her best angle."

"If you didn't tell me... I wouldn't know what to do!" Edie yells at the unseen Chuck. She picks up an ashtray, and throws it in the direction of his voice.

Somewhere off-screen, Wein cackles at his betrayal.

⌘

One of the worst things that can happen to a person who has written about their sexual imaginings free of context, and in a public manner, is having a new partner read them.

It was late in the summer, a 90 degree night. He had just picked me up from work. It was early in our relationship, when we were both excited about each other, and wanted to spend as much time together as possible. (My idealized notion of love: I would fixate on the heartbreak I would feel if he were to suddenly drop dead.) I was starving, and felt gross from the heat. When we got to his house, what I wanted most was to eat, and take a shower. I put something in the microwave, and went upstairs to get cleaned up. While I was taking my clothes off in his bedroom, he came up behind me and pushed me down on the bed. His mouth was like a drain cover leaking steam in my ear. His body on top of mine was all sticky, dead weight. "I want to eat," I said. "And take a shower," "You'll eat when I'm done with you," he said.

He'd told me a few nights before that he'd found an abandoned blog of mine online. I'd told him not to read it, because the writing was old, and not very good. Something I'd written there about an old boyfriend piqued his interest. *He comes through the door like a home invasion fantasy.* "What do you mean there?" he'd asked. "Don't read anymore," I said. "You wouldn't understand." Though I didn't think he would understand, I'd said it as a playful insult. (We transition from the "playful" violence of adolescence, to the less- energy sapping playful insult as adults.)

"First you're going to suck me off, then you're going to beg," he said. This might have been an awkward, yet potentially salvageable scenario, if I hadn't felt so hungry and hot. He got off of me, I suppose for me to kneel, and I got up to tend to my original plan of taking a shower. Grabbing me by the arm, he spun me around, and hit me hard in the face.

Writing this now — years later — in the temperate spring, showered, and fed — it turns me on a bit, as being removed from events often does, but that night, it's hard to explain what it was like to be confronted with someone else's interpretation of my own words.

In fantasies, you are not hungry. Your body does not feel stank from the heat. All everyday human variables are removed, and the circumstances are neutered, almost like Barbie Dolls. The violence is perfect. The "rape" perfect. And your partner isn't revealing something about themselves by assuming to know what it is you want, by potentially exploiting what it is they hope you want.

Fantasies are your own creation. They exist just for you. I don't believe that they are supposed to be experienced, or that they can be. I think fantasy is just the silencing of the voice inside of us that makes us so aware of how complicated and uncomfortable it can be as a human, around other humans. Perhaps love can also do this, provide a safe haven for the awareness of this discomfort, and I don't know.

There was a poem I'd written up at the blog that my boyfriend read that contained this line:

I sought out degradation thinking it would feel like freedom but it always felt like degradation not like freedom at all.

&

In 1988, I heard W. Axl Rose sing/say these words in the Guns N' Roses song, "It's So Easy":

You get nothing for nothing if that's what you do. Turn around bitch I got a use for you. Besides, you ain't got nothing better to do, and I'm bored.

First, remember that you're not in anyway a sexually liberated person, and by that, I mean, come on, this is 1988. You are 12. You're interested in sex in an organic way: you don't have to look at pictures to stir this interest (Al Gore has yet to invent the internet, and all the visual stuff geared towards heterosexual girls in the 80s? Ha! The accessible stuff's all Chippendales), you don't have to read books—though you have found books with passages that evoke certain responses—free of external stimulus, your body is interested, but you're deeply ashamed of having these feelings.

In the future, you will spend a bit of time blaming your parents for this, but eventually you will come to realize it wasn't all them. It would have been nice if they'd offered up a bit of interpretation, a bit of guidance, but parents want to keep their kids kids. This is honorable. They do what they can towards that goal. You can't verbalize these feelings with your friends, and if your friends have these feelings, too, they don't share them with you. All around you, Reagan in the White House, sex is equated with shame. Posters pop up in cities in your area with the words: SILENCE EQUALS DEATH. Other communities struggle with a much more dire consequence of sex shame. When you get older, people from these communities become your heroes.

You and your friend start a notebook called The Rape Book but neither one of you acknowledge to the other what that means. Really, at your age, it could mean almost anything: rape= cute, rape=kiss, rape=go out on a date. Maybe, some 30 years later, when you ask your friend about it, it turns out she is right. Maybe it was all you. Maybe it meant something different to you than it meant to her. Maybe she never went to bed at night dreaming that someone would push her down in the sand, maybe she never felt aroused reading the infamous rape passage in The Clan of the Cave Bear. She never tells you.

In her book *The Argonauts* Maggie Nelson writes:

"If you're looking for sexual tidbits as a female child, and the only ones that present themselves depict child rape or other violations… then your sexuality will form around that fact." (Nelson goes on to mention the infamous rape passage in *Clan of the Cave Bear*.)

A year after starting the notebook with the list of boys' names, I heard Axl Rose sing those words.

Once again:

You get nothing for nothing if that's what you do. Turn around abitch I got a use for you. Besides, you ain't got nothing better to do, and I'm bored.

It was the lyrical version of my fantasies, and it was contemporary. All of the elements were there: I can have what I want, because it's what he wants. He's bored. I'm blameless.

All the names of The Rape Book were people Marie and I knew, except for two. Micky Dolenz, of course. And Axl Rose. I wrote both.

"It's safe to say that most sex involves some form of nostalgia for something," Andy Warhol once said.

I still think, despite it's misogynistic sleaziness, "It's So Easy" is a very sexy song.

ℓ⁇

About a month after our phone conversation, and a few weeks after the visit when I don't see her, Marie texts me. It's my birthday.

4-0, she writes. *Perhaps now is the time to stop writing stories about being a kid.*

Haha, I respond. I've known her too long; there's no hard feelings. *I finished that story without your help. Want to help now, and read it?*

I don't wait for her to respond, and email what I've written.

Later that night, I receive this message:

> *Three things:*
> *1. You know I think you're a good writer, regardless of the subject matter.*
> *2. I don't think I ever used the words "spectator" or "captive audience of one."*
> *3. Did you incorporate Andy Warhol into this just to spite me????*

PLAYING THE DONALD TRUMP GAME

It's funny to me that I can remember Donald Trump so clearly in the 1980s. I was just a kid, but I can. He was like a Swatch watch; he had a big cultural moment. Donald Trump, AIDS, Bernie Goetz, Cabbage Patch Kids, they are all connected in my mind. They are all totems of the Reagan years. "The Donald" — the youngish tycoon championed for his business acumen, and his disco lifestyle, his platinum blonde wife with the exotic name, *Ivana*, at his side. He was a camp interest, but one with an underlying message attached: *Greed is good. Robin Leach will interview you in your gold-plated hot tub.*

Trump and the AIDS crisis are forever linked in my mind, and now the conflation seems prescient, almost psychic. My greatest fear for his presidency, besides a more impulsive version of the end of times scenario laid out in the Genesis "Land of Confusion" video, is how the already vulnerable in this country will be treated.

When I first became aware of the existence of Donald Trump, I was twelve. My friend Gwen had moved to the area with her family the year before. She lived in a big, modern house with huge picture windows, and a fake deer out in the yard. The rumor was that her mom had modelled the house's design on the home of another girl in our grade; that one day she had dropped Gwen off there, and went back to Gwen's dad, and said, *I want that house.* It was probably true; the houses were almost mirror images. As the contestants chant as they spin the wheel on the game show, "Wheel of Fortune" — *Big money! Big money!* As F. Scott Fitzgerald famously wrote, "the rich are different from you and me." There is a bias that leans towards them being better.

Nobody knew what Gwen's father did for a living. Something that involved a leather swivel chair in a private office inside the house that we weren't supposed to go into, (though we did, giddy to use his fancy phone with its multiple lines), and constantly changing business partners. Something that involved her family moving a lot, and her dad buying up real estate, and setting up bank accounts for his use in Gwen and her siblings' names.

My family was poor: my father was an immigrant, a house painter when he worked, and my mother was a secretary. One night, while I was spending the night at Gwen's house, her father said to me, "I hope you enjoy all the food that I pay for," as I took a bite out of some take-out he'd brought back to the house. My family wasn't *that* poor. I wasn't there because I was starving.

My mother, who had no private office, or swivel chair, never said anything like that to Gwen when she ate at our house. I remember her father's mouth as he spoke, the chewed food still visible inside it. I remember wanting to disappear, wanting to hide, but what I wanted the most was to pull out a wallet full of hundred dollar bills, and have my father materialize carrying a briefcase, and wearing a suit and tie. At twelve, how do you respond to a comment like that? How do you refute the sting of it?

For her birthday that year, Gwen really wanted the Donald Trump board game. It was expensive for a board game, and came in a box the size of a phone book, with "The Donald's" face on the top, the same picture that was on the cover of his bestselling book *The Art of the Deal* which was written by someone else, not "The Donald," because as I would learn once I got older, success means you can outsource the story of your success. I was going to get the game for her. She wanted it badly, and it's fun to get something for someone you like, especially when you know how much they want it. This is something people without a lot of money know about acutely.

I had to wait until after Christmas, which was fine, because her birthday was right after Christmas. I bought it for her at a local gift shop, with the money I got from my grandparents for the holiday. My grandparents owned the house that my family lived in, had given my mother the car that she drove. Unlike sibling hand-me-downs, an ugly sweater, these were survival hand-me-downs. (I used to think that the reason families gave their kids names that began with the same letter was to save money on the L.L Bean monogrammed sweaters that were popular at the time.) My father drove a Ford Pinto. When he worked, he kept his paint supplies in the back.

If you are a poor person, what kind of poor person would you identify as?

a. proud
b. ashamed
c. grateful
d. angry

If you are not a poor person, how do you think the poor should feel?

a. proud
b. ashamed
c. grateful
d. angry

My mother wasn't supposed to be so needy. She'd gone to Catholic high school, she'd gone to college. But she dropped out a semester before graduation. She dropped out because she'd believed in something, and wanted to dedicate her life to it. Perhaps it was easier for her not to resist that passion because of the safety net of her parents, but my grandparents were not rich. My grandfather never graduated high school; after serving in the military during

World War II, he became an insurance agent, thanks to a local man who helped the children of Italian immigrants find careers. (The altruism of this local man aided three generations of my family.) My grandfather did well at his job, and my mother grew up middle class, but this only increased the sting of her dropping out. She would have been the first person in her family to graduate.

The house that I grew up in, the house that my grandparents owned, was the same house that my mother had grown up in, only it was in a state of decay. There was a gas station next door, and the street it was on had become a major thoroughfare. The fence around the property was falling down, and drunken patrons from the bar across the street would sometimes pass out in my dad's car. They'd come to the next day with splotches of regret on their clothes from the cans of paint he kept on the backseat.

My grandparents were pissed at my mother. They were pissed at her for thinking with her heart, and not with her head, meaning, her purse, not thinking of her financial future. My grandmother's side of the family was Irish, and my mother had dropped out of college because she wanted to help liberate Ireland from English rule. When people talk about the activism of the 1960s and the 70s, they don't talk much about the Irish Freedom movement, but that was where my mother threw her heart, and lost her wallet, and that is how she met my father, an Irish immigrant from Dublin. The children born of their union, myself and my siblings, led my grandparents to reconcile with my mother, and save us from abject poverty, but they did not save us in any way that satisfied my twelve year old self.

My grandparent's gifts allowed us to pass as lower middle class in a well-to-do area. Look at the language: "to pass." The true color of my economic skin, the birth sex of my economic gender: poor. Their generosity granted us protection from the elements, and the possibility of travel in a car that was not a Ford Pinto, but I wasn't in a place where I could feel gratitude for these gifts. They lacked flash, socio-economic glow. I felt shame about my family's economic circumstances, and the signifiers that I knew betrayed them. To compensate, I fantasized, and lied. Donald Trump subscribes to the idea that if you repeat a lie enough, it will become the truth, but my family's economic circumstances didn't change. This mendacious alchemy didn't work for us.

What Gwen's father probably meant with his comment about the food was that he was sick of paying for me when Gwen wanted me to come along when they did bigger-budget things, like went skiing, or maybe what he really wanted was to hear me say *thank you* while genuflecting. I know I said it while standing, every time, because I was raised to have good manners, to always say *please* and *thank you*. Please is a strange word when you spend too much time thinking about it. Inherent to its utility is the idea that there is a sweetening that occurs when a person is willing to acknowledge their lesser place in the power dynamic. You must tread lightly though, the mechanics are so delicate, that even giving lip service to the revelation could get you labelled an ingrate. *Please* is the sadism of gratitude. *Thank you* the masochism.

Often, I'd be at Gwen's house when her family would spontaneously come up with the idea of doing something — one of the perks of having money is the ability to be spontaneous, to play with it, and because of my presence, I'd end up absorbed into their plans. At my house, all of our spontaneous activities took planning. My friendship with his daughter was real. It wasn't about take-out. It wasn't about skiing. I still have no idea what it costs to ski. The only time I ever went was with their family.

It's strange to think about the insecurities that must plague men like Gwen's father, men who present themselves *bigly*. They like that word, too, bigly ("big league"); they also have a weakness for the expression "big time." Why do bigly men who have access to so much, still feel a need to degrade those who don't, to humiliate them, to remind them when they are being given something, or twist it around, claiming that something has been taken from them? It might not be worth much, but I remember what the take-out was, that night at Gwen's. The straw that broke her bigly father's back was chicken from KFC.

If you don't have better coping skills, in a primitive bid to rid yourself of what you've been made to feel, you might try to pass it on to someone else. I remember me, and another girl like me, another girl with a run down house, seeking each other out, and taunting each other. Saying, *You're poor. No, you're poor.* Which is really saying, you're the degraded one. Not me. Chasing each other around the schoolyard. *No, your life is of lesser value. You say "please" more.* Something existed in our lives that we knew we should be ashamed of, that we knew made us vulnerable. Growing up, I dreaded four words, and my mother said them all the time. *We can't afford it.* I feared that she might say them around someone else, that someone might hear her.

Yesterday I was at Subway. I go there often, and know the staff, all Spanish-speaking immigrants, who make what I call degradation wages, as opposed to minimum wages, or the laughingly dishonest, honest wages. It was a Friday night, and I watched as a blonde woman with a newscaster haircut and three young girls in her charge all placed their complicated orders, as if ordering at some kind of specialty delicatessen, when not laughing about some joke on their cell phones, ignoring the employees' questions of cheese qualification.

She wanted a foot long, on two different kinds of bread, which demands that the rules of Subway sandwich making be bended — with provolone cheese, no, with pepper jack cheese; she was indecisive on every ingredient, as she encouraged the young girls to be. The line grew longer behind them; the woman carried on, almost obliviously, but it wasn't that she was truly oblivious, it was that she was comfortable. She was *comfortable* making others uncomfortable on the long march towards getting whatever it was she wanted. The employees kept their heads down. I knew that they were simmering with rage, I was simmering with rage watching, but in order to get your degradation wages, you must keep your mouth closed. What

I wanted most in that moment was to free them from what held them there, heads down, unable to tell this ridiculous woman what she deserved to hear: *Today ma'am, you can eat shit.* After paying, studying her receipt to make sure she hadn't been overcharged, the woman put no tip in the plastic box by the register, not that a tip would have disinfected the exchange, but she paid with cash, and certainly could have. I looked out in the parking lot, and watched her get into her big SUV with its *Make America Great Again* bumper sticker. *Nothing taken from me today,* she probably thought. I mention this woman for one reason: one of the employees and I had talked about the election in the weeks before November 8th. One of the men who had made her sandwiches had told me he wanted Donald Trump to win.

Why? I'd asked him. *Why?*

He'd said something about Hillary Clinton wanting to make college affordable for everyone — the kind of lofty ideal that comes up during a campaign, and then often never goes anywhere once the candidate is elected — and how would the country pay for that? I'd wondered to myself, how come this man wouldn't want affordable college, if not for himself, then for his friends, or family? I couldn't imagine his taxes would be that much affected, he seemed to me to be the kind of person affordable tuition would most benefit. And anyway, this far off dream of egalitarian education was enough to get him to throw his support behind Donald Trump? The man was Spanish-speaking, he was an immigrant. Wouldn't the normal rules of the universe say he'd find Trump and all his campaign postures abhorrent? Two white men were standing in line next to me as we had the exchange, they'd actually started it. They made little whooping sounds indicating that they agreed with what the employee was saying.

You may never be bigly, but you can take measures to negate the shame that you are made to feel because of it. For the sake of your ego, you can keep your head down; never look the entitled person in the eye. You can turn away from those most like you, because your affiliation with them might give you away. You can try to blend amongst those who might point you out and put you down: adopt what they wear, how they speak. Who they despise.

It wasn't just the employee. It was the owner of the liquor store, who says he's faced housing discrimination because he's Muslim. The woman from AA with diabetes, who suffers from mental illness and has experienced sexual assault. I noticed a phenomenon during this election. Vulnerable, marginalized people supporting Donald Trump — or at least claiming publicly to support Donald Trump. Groups of people he had maligned, or implied wouldn't be so welcome in the America he would be making great again. I think some of those people supported him because they didn't want to think of themselves as part of the population he was actively denigrating; they didn't want to think of themselves as marginalized, as the people he was calling "losers," or "rapists," or "Miss Piggy," or threatening to deport. It was as if by supporting him they were saying, "That's not me — that's another group of people, and here's the ultimate proof it's not me, I'm saying fuck them, too." I think they supported him out of shame. I also think some of them projected onto Trump as a realization of the bigly dream: all the gold-plated goodies great wealth can buy, the attractive spouse, really a revisiting of all the elements that had bought Trump to fame in the 80s.

Supporting Trump was about the things they wanted for themselves, and things they wanted to believe about themselves. It was also about the things they didn't want to believe about themselves: one being that he and his supporters were talking about them. Perhaps it wasn't shame so much, as it was fear. What is shame anyway, but the internalized fear of being found out?

The first time I was on government assistance, I was nineteen. I had blue hair, and was part of a punk rock subculture. Receiving it felt defiant in the face of my childhood, and the shame I'd felt then. But there's a fetishization of poverty that occurs in young, white artistic subcultures, and it happens because most of them fully expect to someday transcend their circumstances. Governmental assistance is treated like a novelty, an accessory, something cosmetic, like blue hair. When I received it in my 30s, my hair it's natural color, no longer a part of any subculture but that of a single, working-poor parent, those old feelings of shame could have easily returned. Gwen's father's voice and words belonged to the every big man, and he loved talking about me: on the television, in newspaper editorials, on the campaign trail, in conversations I overheard, and in comments said to my face when they didn't realize they were talking about me: *I hope you enjoy all that I pay for.* It's a testament to the very real need of the poor, the constant abuse they are made to suffer. How they are constantly made to have to prove that need for critique. For the poor, it's a constant economy of degradation.

I've written about very personal things, but it feels like a different kind of revelation to write about money, because it's the measure in so many minds — even better ones — of success, and failure. In the arts, where monetary rewards are slim, success is gauged then not by actual dollars, but by proximity to actual dollars. Are you a *paid* writer? Do you have an *agent* — which is just asking does some bigly person *think* they can sell you? Your price might be pennies, but there's prestige in just having a price.

My child is eleven, and reminds me of myself at twelve. I have been unable to shield him. He watches the home renovation channel on TV, and I know what he's doing, he's dreaming. At times, I've heard him lying to his friends. No one seems to consider what the big student loan debt confession sounds like to a lot of people: a humble-brag. *Yes, I have this debt, but I'm moving on up.*

It hurts me to write this. Before my father and my mother gave up their activism to raise kids, and work jobs for not much money that degraded their very real intelligence, they had both been very good at harnessing their passion: their want for Irish freedom. Free of intellectual stimulation in his work, my father floundered. He drank. He didn't work for long stretches of time. My father died when I was seventeen, and my clearest memories of him are all from periods when he wasn't working: whenever

I'd stay home from school sick, we'd watch movies together, on the couch. A lot of his employers were wealthy, and their material success must have made him feel smaller, less than. Unemployed, he spent a lot of time at the library, because if there was anything my father would have wanted for himself, it would have been a college education. There one day, he met a reporter working on a story about the Irish in America. He interviewed my father for the piece, I imagine, based on the stories my father must have told him in their initial conversations — because in America, my father had started to tell tales. He'd said he'd been a professor in New York City, that he'd graduated from Trinity College. In scheme of things, his lies weren't superficial, they were humble. They were lies that said take me seriously, *see me*, here's my phony credentials. It makes me so sad, that that shame can still get you, even when you know better, even when you've dedicated years of your life to revolution.

I bought Gwen the Trump game. The slogan that had sold it in commercials at the time was "It's not whether you win or lose, it's whether you win." Winning, was of course, amassing wealth and properties, the attributes that made Trump so famous in the 1980s. Considering that he has no political experience, I believe they're the same attributes that have made him so popular now — his wealth, combined with the knack for cruelty that he has shown in the media, and out on the campaign trail. I think this is the real divide in this country: the social principles of empathy, vs the social principles of greed. The funny thing is, they need not be mutually exclusive. It's clear what side of the divide House Speaker Paul Ryan is on when he says children of poor families don't want free lunch at school as much as they want "dignity." It's capitalism writ cruel, and I fear that the upcoming cruelty is being anticipated as much as the guard change.

I can't remember Gwen and I actually playing the Trump game. What I do remember, is my joy, my sense of pride, at being able to give it to her as a gift. A few years later, I spied the cover of the box in a corner of her large walk-in closet — I caught a glimpse of "The Donald's" face. Though it was only a few years later, the early 1990s, what Donald Trump represented already seemed like a relic ideology, from a distant era. *I can't believe she still has it,* I thought to myself. *Or that I bought it. The 80s. What an ugly time.*

VAGARIES OF THE DEMIMONDE

"It just seems strange. Lou Reed dies, but I live? It doesn't seem right."

Dr. Oswald looked confused. He furrowed his brow.

"Oh right, right. The musician. It's unfortunate, but for some patients, previous treatments make the new treatments impossible. His case was so far advanced. He'd had cancer, and a liver transplant."

Dr. Oswald put down the pen he was holding, and studied me for a moment. "Most patients mention Pamela Anderson," he said.

Pamela Anderson. "The Poison Pin-Up." I loved her, and would have mentioned her, eventually.

In 2002, she'd revealed to the world she had Hepatitis C, a grimy, blood- borne pathogen, contrary to her healthy, blonde, Hugh Hefner-endorsed brand of sexiness. Though, through her relationship with Tommy Lee, of Motley Crue, and her barbed-wire tattoo (which she'd gotten in the mid- 1990s, before tattoos were ubiquitous), Anderson had always had an edginess that most Playboy Playmates lacked. Courtney Love of all people had once referred to Anderson as "Dirty Pam." I'd sometimes use the media's nickname for Anderson for myself: I, too, was a Poison Pin-up.

But according to Dr. Oswald, not for much longer.

"In six months, you'll be Hepatitis C-free," he said. "Cured! In the last six months, I've cured close to sixty patients. Cured! I want to see you smile!"

He waited. I responded with a weak smile.

"I want to see you dance! Come on! I'm curing you!"

"I'm grateful," I said. "I'm just not overly demonstrative. I like to play it cool. It's the influence of Lou Reed."

It was annoying that Dr. Oswald kept saying *he* was curing me. The medication *would be* curing me. Dr. Oswald was a man I would be seeing for ten minutes, once a month, with a pen.

Yes, this was a pivotal moment in my life, a life-changing one, but Dr. Oswald was yet another man telling me I should smile.

&

The phone calls from the black-ops pharmacy started a few days later. I was on two medications: Sovaldi and Ribavirin. As Dr. Oswald had thoroughly impressed upon me (almost as if I should be honored), the Sovaldi cost $800 *a pill*. The black-ops pharmacy only sent me two weeks' worth at a time, fourteen pills, in the event I might drop dead in the interim, and the government of the state that I lived in would be out the thousands of dollars in already dispensed medication.

I kind of couldn't believe that "The Man" was willing to shell out so much money for me. For most of my early adult life, I'd been what fiscal conservatives (to put them kindly) considered to be (to put me kindly) a drain on the system, in and out of rehab, hardly paying any income taxes at all. Now, I made less than $20,000 a year, and wrote essays (and a book) about sex work, addiction, and my appreciation of artistic reprobates. I'd had a Charles Manson scrapbook in junior high. I'd joined the Social Workers Party in high school. There had been no point in my life where I hadn't been Marxist-leaning and/or fucked. But if my Hepatitis C advanced, say to the Lou Reed-stages of cirrhosis, then liver cancer, it could carry an even heavier price tag. My state government viewed treating me now as cost effective in the long run.

The black-ops pharmacy was very on top of my medication needs. Every other week, I'd get a phone call.

"Hello. It's ****** Pharmacy. Could I have your name, and date of birth please?"

I'd give it.

"Your personal pin number?"

I'd give it.

"Your high school boyfriend's mom's sister's babysitter's dad's last name?"

I'd give it.

Then they'd arrange the drop off.

Sometimes this was a hassle, because I had to be there to sign for the medication. They wouldn't leave it, and no one else could sign for it. If something went wrong with the first delivery attempt, they'd set up a second delivery for the next day, with a scheduled time. They would never just do it the more efficient second way first.

It was an amazing procession to be a part of, all of it for my liver — the pharmacy and the delivery service with their outstretched hands shaking the branches of the over $100,000 money tree that was the total cost of my three months of treatment.

All self-deprecation aside, what had made my Hep C treatment possible, what had made my Hep C *cure* possible, was the state that I live in had agreed to cover the cost for low-income patients. Most states don't, or fight it first, requiring patients to have advanced liver disease, or to pass invasive drug tests. People die waiting to be approved for treatment that they would have had better access to had they lived a few states to the west, or a few states to the north, or in a poorer country, like India. In India, Sovaldi sells for $4.00 a pill.

My access to a cure for my Hepatitis C came down to one thing: the vagaries of geography.

೧

It's crass, but when people ask me about my experience with Hepatitis C, and my experience with the new treatment, I sometimes say, "Easy come, easy go."

I tried to keep a journal while I was taking the medication, but what was happening in the world figured into it more predominantly than what was happening in my body.

We need to update the aphorism "there are no atheists in a foxhole." Wars are no longer fought that way. There are no atheists in a school shooting. There are no atheists in a Paris nightclub attack.

Charlie Sheen has come out as HIV+. Talking heads on TV are wondering if "Tiger Blood" was always a cryptic allusion to his serostatus.

I had never had any side effects I could identify with having Hepatitis. I just knew that the virus was there in my body, lurking. I had a child two years after being diagnosed, and to my amazement, after a surprise visit from La Leche League, learned I was able to breastfeed that child, something that my obstetrician hadn't even known. I experienced fatigue sometimes, but who doesn't? Life is often physically and emotionally exhausting. I had no stomach ailments, no nausea, no "Coca-Cola colored urine."

The first few days I took the medication, I felt a pronounced sense of tiredness, but that was it. It was unbelievably painless, easy, and uneventful. My life was not disrupted. I'd watched a boyfriend take interferon treatments in 2004, and that had been horrible. There were days he looked grey-green, rubbery and Gumby-like. He couldn't handle it, and we started getting high a month into his treatment. Sometimes, we'd shoot up with his sanitized interferon syringes.

I hadn't gotten Hepatitis C from him, but we'd been together when I learned I'd had it. By 2004, I'd been using heroin for ten years, and most of the drug users I knew had it. I'd been in and out of treatment by that point, and found myself surrounded by a more seasoned breed of addict: the hardcore. All of my friends who had used for a little bit, then picked themselves up, and went off to college, had done exactly that. They'd been replaced by those who might never get it together, who had caught diseases, worked shitty jobs, and lived with their mothers when not in jail or halfway houses. I'd become one in their ranks.

In spite of the necessary medical warnings, it's very hard to get Hepatitis C from sex. Some doctors describe it as being virtually impossible. I know who I got Hepatitis C from, which I only mention because I'm an oddly sentimental person. In a sense, it was like she was there in my body, waiting for the right moment to hit me, just as she'd been the last time I'd seen her.

Whenever I'd spend too long thinking about my virus, I'd always end up thinking about Callie.

ᕳᕲ

It was near the end of the 20th century; I was in my very early twenties. I stopped paying income tax in 1997. I'd been an IV drug user since 1993. Needle use is an easy line to cross once you get over your childhood doctor office hang-ups. Drug addiction in a lot of ways is an extended exposure therapy to all the things you once feared as a child.

I'm not proud, but even though I grew up in the 1990s, very aware of AIDS, I could be sloppy when it came to always using clean needles. The precautions that I took when having to share them were usually contingent on the desperation I felt. If the desperation to get high wasn't overwhelming, and there was bleach available, I would clean the needle I was sharing with bleach. But if the desperation to get high was less manageable, I would clean the needle I was sharing with just water. I had started using heroin when I was in high school. I got high with a close group of friends who I'd grown up with, using needles that my best friend's mother had stored away in the basement after going through treatment for cancer. It wasn't science, but we knew each other's exposure risks, because we were each other's exposure risks. It was dangerous and stupid, but as a group, we were contained. Once I ventured out into the wider world, this openness to being lackadaisical would become a problem.

My drug use is at the nexus of so many different threads in my life: punk rock, sex work, Lou Reed and past-epoch romanticism — in New York City all these divergent threads would meet. And I suppose, the end result was Hepatitis C. Perhaps this is what happens when you move to New York City looking to bleat a corpse.

If I couldn't live in New York City in the late 1970s, I would live there like it was still 1978.

છ૭

I once got into an argument with a drug counselor about whether or not IV drugs could be done recreationally. She said they couldn't. I said they could. Recreation (to me, as well as Webster's) is *fun*. Recreation (to me, as well as Webster's) is *friends*. IV drug use will never be viewed in those terms: it makes people too squeamish. It's too ugly. It will always be seen as the end of the road, the last stop before death. And while this is often very true, there is also friendship in it, there is humor, there is fun. IV drug users aren't just human pin cushions with bloody walls. "Junky chic" will never involve the actual needle, just the greasy, skanky sallowness that comes along with it, because friendship, humor, fun, is never *chic*. Just ask Anna Wintour.

Callie and I shared needles, but we shared a lot of other things, too.

છ૭

I met Callie through her boyfriend Juan. Juan was someone who I'd see at punk rock shows when I was in high school. He was older, and somewhat intimidating, with vulgar tattoos on his hands and neck. He was a man of few words, unless he was drunk, then he was incomprehensible. I was just learning about drugs then, while Juan had already committed years of his life to them. I didn't know him well, but when I moved to New York City, he was already living there. He became one of the people I'd buy drugs from. When he and his girlfriend, Callie, were evicted from where they'd been living, and sleeping in cheap hotel rooms, and on the street, I agreed to let them stay with me. I liked the idea of having an in-house drug dealer. That Juan came with human baggage in the form of Callie, I agreed to suck up.

But the more I got to know Callie, the more I liked her. The more I got to know Juan, the less I liked him. The first night they stayed with me, Juan tried to come onto me as Callie slept in the other room. Callie was two years older than me. She had moved to New York City to go to art school, but had dropped out a few semesters short of graduation. She had short black hair that she wore in a Coco Chanel-style bob, and even while she and Juan were without a place to stay, always managed to look elegant and sophisticated. She was the first person I'd ever met who wore clothes by designers like Givenchy and Commes des Garcon; designers so far from my point of reference, that at first I thought she was talking about bands I'd never heard of. While they'd been short on money, Juan had taken some of her clothes and sold them in the East Village. I'd listen as she described what she'd lost, enamored of the delicate language that she used. It was like she was talking about flaky pastries at a bakery.

Within a month of coming to my apartment, Juan was arrested for selling heroin to an undercover cop.

Juan was going to prison. He had an arrest history, and no one to bail him out before his court date, but what he seemed the most concerned with was having Callie smuggle him drugs when she came to visit. After her first visit with Juan, she came back to the apartment with an elaborate plan as to how she would bring him heroin the next time.

You are crazy, I said. *Crazy. You are going to get caught, and if you don't get caught, he'll ask you to do it again, and then you'll get caught.*

I wondered if Juan would have preferred that Callie be in jail, too. Despite his own cheating (and cheating attempts), he was extremely possessive of her, and exuded machismo. It was clear from his collect calls that his paranoia about their relationship was escalating.

I gave Callie an ultimatum.

If you bring him drugs, you can't stay here.

I wonder if she felt confident to make the decision that she did because of our burgeoning relationship. I could become her focus. I could fill her Juan-shaped hole.

Callie dropped the idea of bringing Juan drugs, and we fell into a period of best-friend bliss.

❧

If Callie had an Achilles heel more detrimental than her drug use, it was men. No, it was love in general. Even before Juan, Callie had a history of making bad decisions while drunk on the idea of love. Her love was big and dramatic, like a Lana Turner movie from the 1950s, with fights on street corners, and life or death proclamations. Juan wasn't the first man she'd dropped out of school for, nor was he the first for whom she'd cut off all communication with her family. He wasn't the first she'd lived with on the street, and he wouldn't be the last.

And like Lana Turner in those films, Callie dressed well, in garments with clean lines, in muted hues — grey, beige, and black — adding an element of noir ambiance to the pathos.

❧

We stopped accepting Juan's phone calls. Once in awhile, she or I would answer his letters, which always included requests asking that either one of us send him naked pictures. (We'd heard from friends that other women were already visiting him in prison.) Juan's supplier had a crush on Callie, and said he wanted to help her "get on her feet," and fronted her drugs to sell. Instead, we did them. Around this time, pharmacies started to get tougher about selling needles without a prescription. Instead of schlepping down to the needle exchange during their hours of operation, you had been able to go into select pharmacies, and by either giving a name, and date of birth, or showing an ID, they would sell you syringes. These pharmacies became harder to find, so sometimes, Callie and I would share. I tried to be thorough about cleaning the needle. I knew she gotten Hepatitis C from sharing needles with an ex-boyfriend, but there were times I wanted to get high so badly.

Callie got on methadone, and I decided to get on it, too. We'd spend hours walking around the East Village after going to our treatment programs. We'd go to Kim's Video and to See Hear, the zine store. We'd browse the small boutiques, looking for Callie's clothes that Juan had sold. They only bought on consignment, meaning the item had to be sold in the store before you got paid for it. We decided then that Juan must have sold her clothes on the street. The idea of her clothes spread out on the sidewalk for pedestrians to paw seemed to genuinely pain her.

But we'd spend most of our time in Tompkins Square Park, with the addicts and alcoholics who decamped all day there. Some of the park regulars had played bit parts in the 1970s and 80s punk and no wave scene. I loved listening to their stories about drumming for Johnny Thunders, or acting in the early films of Eric Mitchell and Jim Jarmusch, or what had *really happened* the night Nancy Spungen died. Over the next few years, my favorite Tompkins

Square Park storytellers would both die from complications related to Hepatitis C.

Callie and I were never put off by the downtrodden, but she was much more friendly and tolerant of the transit punk rock travelers who also hung out in and around the park. I liked to imagine that we were part of a larger, more romantic tradition, something I couldn't see in their aggressive panhandling, and hostile pitbulls. In them I saw a ruthlessness born of desperation.

As she'd done with expensive clothing, Callie introduced me to expensive make-up, and we'd go shoplifting at Sephora. At night, we'd go see friends' bands play at CBGB's, or heroes like Lydia Lunch at Life, or Kembra Pfahler at Coney Island High, or we'd listen to Richard Hell read from his work at St. Mark's Poetry Project.

One day, I saw Lou Reed walking down St. Marks Place. It wasn't lost on me that St. Marks had been the site of the Electric Circus, "New York's ultimate mixed-media pleasure dome," where Reed had played with the Velvet Underground. St. Mark's had also been the scene of the eponymous Sally's decline in his song, "Sally Can't Dance."

"Lou Reed is the guy that gave dignity and poetry and rock n' roll to smack, speed, homosexuality, sadomasochism…" Lester Bangs said.

I'd moved to New York City because I'd believed in that dignity, and had immediately thrown myself into the demimonde.

For my birthday, Callie gave me a card with an inscription that read, "To my sister." The message was pre-printed, in someone else's words, but the sentiment was true.

We were like sisters. *Demimondaines.*

❧

If the closeness of my relationship with Callie can be measured in bodily fluids:

For his birthday, we had a threesome with our friend Paul. As I gave him a blowjob, Callie went down on me. After they had sex, Paul rolled over to my side of the bed. Something about this struck me as too much, though. I grabbed a bottle of water from the nightstand, and dumped it on his penis, first.

Callie thought she had an infection, but didn't want to go the gynecologist, if it wasn't necessary. She put a finger inside herself, and held it up to my face.

Do you think I need to go? she asked.

I wasn't sure.

She put her finger under my nose.

No, I said, *You're fine.*

☙

I was working as an escort, and Callie said she'd worked as a dancer. We would sometimes do outcalls together, but Callie only wanted to work with me, as a team, which wasn't always possible. This was our only steady source of income, and if she couldn't work with me, Callie started making excuses not to go. She'd say she was sick, or had gotten her period; she never offered to show me the blood, or the snot. I hated doing it, too. I still have dread dreams about it: where most people I know have the dread dream where they have to take a big test for school, and aren't prepared for it, I have the dread dream where I have to go back to work as an escort. Callie had enjoyed her freedom from Juan, but she'd also been comfortable in his chains. Though he hadn't done it well, often leaving her dope sick, or ignorant as to his whereabouts, Juan and her other boyfriends had taken care of her according to standards she had accepted. I didn't see it as care; I saw it as laying claim. I cared about her, but I also expected an equal division of labor. There was nothing Lana Turner about our relationship.

In order to cut down on expenses, we both went up ungodly amounts on our methadone. It was futile for us to do heroin, since we couldn't feel it, but we still tried.

Then one day, while standing outside my drug treatment program, I discovered Xanax.

And Callie discovered Perdition.

☙

Perdition was the perfect name for him. *Hell,* only said smartly. If anyone ever came with a flashing LED light that said "Warning: Preening Loser," it was him.

Callie was a beautiful girl. She'd never had a hard time meeting men, she just never had much resistance to one who showed interest in her first, and had drugs.

Perdition (of all things) looked like a Hasidic Jew. He had wiry black hair, long, dark sideburns, and a colonial times beard. He cultivated darkness and gloom, wore it, and fine-tuned it as a weapon he shot from his mouth. His nihilism didn't wear him down; on the contrary, it invigorated him. If he saw a flower growing from a crack in the pavement, he would pick up his boot and stomp on it. He was like a Nietzschean cartoon character. He reminded me of both Leopold and Loeb. I suspected he was probably gay.

He was also a homeless heroin addict. He had ended up in New York City after hopping trains from somewhere in the middle of the country, somewhere oppressively religious. Callie had met him in Tompkins Square Park, where he'd been selling drugs. Their relationship moved fast. Faster than the Xanax in my brain allowed me to fully comprehend at the time. I knew that Perdition was obnoxious, but because he had drugs, I didn't mind when Callie first brought him back to the apartment. But the more time I spent around him, it became clear that his drugs were not enough to warrant his presence in our lives. I don't think he even liked Callie. I think he liked having a place to stay, and a woman at his side to insult.

Nights I'd go to work, and come home to Perdition's *Natural Born Killers* votaries camped out in my living room, his gross boots outside my bedroom door, and my dogs hiding in the closet. He had zero respect for me, and less than zero for Callie. He would degrade her in front of his park-bench coterie with critiques of their sexual activities, what he liked for her to do, and what she did that he didn't like. He didn't seem to understand nor care that the apartment was mine. He was racist, homophobic, and misogynistic — but the worst part was that he was smart, and fast. I am often good with a fiery insult in a loved one's defense, but under the influence of Xanax, I wasn't working at full-brain capacity. I couldn't even properly defend us in my own home.

He had to go.

But the worst part, the real worst part, was watching Callie try to defend him.

"He's different when he's not around his friends," she'd say.

No. The real worst part was listening to Callie denigrate me as she stumped for him.

"He's just like that because he knows you don't like him. You haven't given him a chance. If you did, you'd see that you have things in common."

No. The only thing we had in common, besides drugs, was my interest in Charles Manson as a juvenile; that interest had passed. Perdition was a grown man holding tight to the fascination.

Was it the drugs? Was it the access to them that he provided that made her so willing to degrade herself? Was it me not yet willing to acknowledge that we were already degrading ourselves anyway—most nights when we went to work—so what was one more asshole, anyway? It made me think about her relationship with Juan. I'd never told her about the night he'd come onto me. Would she have just blamed me if I had?

Early one morning, Callie and Perdition got up to go to Tompkins Square Park. Once they were outside the building, I opened my bedroom window, and threw out Perdition's coat.

"You're not coming back!" I yelled.

"Not you, Callie!" I said, registering the scowl on her face. "You can come back. But not him."

Perhaps our relationship was big and dramatic.

Perdition yelled something up at me, but his words are lost to posterity.

Callie's hands rose up to her shoulders, in tight little balls. Then she separated her fingers, so just the middle ones stood.

She flipped me off, and picked up Perdition's coat.

Then they continued walking down the street.

༖

Fine. If that's the way you want it, I said to no one. I went to Callie's area of the closet to pack up her things, but found the space already cleared, and most of her clothes gone. She'd been complaining about the weight she'd put on being on methadone, but I couldn't imagine her actually selling her clothes. I'd noticed that she'd been dressing more like Perdition. She'd been wearing a Rammstein t-shirt of his — a band he liked solely because of their association with the killers at Columbine. There were swatches of fabric from a Vivienne Westwood skirt on the floor. I'd seen patches of the same material on Perdition's coat. He'd obviously cut it up to make some kind of embellishment.

Getting her things together took all of two minutes. I got dressed, went to my drug treatment program, bought some Xanax, and came home.

Somehow, I managed to avoid seeing her downtown, and she never came for the little she'd left behind. I assumed that they were either sleeping in cheap hotel rooms, or on the street. My anger towards her turned into resentment. The Xanax didn't calm my feelings. To anyone willing to listen, I spoke of Callie, and her patheticness.

Then the mail started. Colton Burgess had been ticketed for drinking in the park. Colton Burgess had been taken by disco bus to Beth Israel, and owed the hospital thousands of dollars. The bill had an itemized line for Narcan. Obviously Colton Burgess had overdosed. Colton Burgess was Perdition. I was sure Callie had suggested using my address. It reminded me of when she and I would buy needles, before pharmacy sales had become more restrictive. Out of pure pettiness, we would sometimes give the pharmacy counter person the name of someone we didn't like for the label that went on the syringe bag. *Sometimes* we would say we were someone we didn't like. Sometimes we would say we were Rosie O'Donnell.

A few weeks later, I overdosed on a combination of Xanax and methadone. I was supposed to go to my mother's house for the weekend, and when I didn't show up, and my mother couldn't get me on the phone, she sent my sister who lived on Long Island to investigate. The landlord let her in, and she found me naked on the couch in my living room, my dogs guarding my knocked-out form. My sister called for an ambulance, and dressed me quickly in a t-shirt and a pair of leopard print leggings. When I came to at the hospital, I became fixated on the leggings. Whose were they? Where had they had come from?

Since the hospital couldn't take my word for it that it hadn't been a suicide attempt, I had a crisis volunteer sitting with me in my room at all times. I didn't want to wear the inexplicable leggings any longer, and the volunteer helped me change out of them, and into a hospital gown.

"I want to throw them out," I said. "My family is bringing me more clothes tomorrow."

"Are you sure?" the volunteer asked, holding them up. "They are ugly as sin, but the label says they're Christian Dior."

❧

While I was in the hospital, a doctor noted the high levels of ALT and the low levels of proteins in my blood.

It could be from the overdose, but have you ever been tested for Hepatitis C? he asked.

No, I said.

I took a blood test, and got an appointment for a follow up visit, in a week, at a private practice. I would get the test results then.

When I came for my appointment, the doctor's office was a madhouse, the waiting room filled with indigent patients, all on Medicaid, like myself. After 90 minutes of waiting, I finally got to see the doctor. He gave me a quick once over, poking me a few times with his fingers on my right side, and told me to schedule another appointment.

Well, do I have it? I asked.

Have what? he said, impatiently.

Hepatitis C, I answered.

You have to take the antibody test, he said.

I know, I answered. *I did.*

Oh, he said. He opened one of the many identical folders he was carrying under his arm, and moved around some papers.

Uh… You're fine, he said. *But make sure to schedule another appointment.*

Was it even my folder? Could he even remember my name? The reality was, I wasn't ready to deal with it. I didn't schedule another appointment. I turned his sketchiness into a reprieve.

☙

End Scene:

I am in Tompkins Square Park, and so is Callie. It's early winter, and I've stopped by the park with the disgusting man I get my Xanax from, in spite of my overdose, who I now call my boyfriend, so he will just give me the Xanax for free. Callie is wearing something ridiculous: a long sleeve shirt of some band who she'd normally find appalling —Marilyn Manson, or Slipknot, and striped bondage pants, obviously a desperate outfit made up of someone else's clothes. I mention this not to rub it in, but because the image is indelible in my mind. Something bad happened: Perdition did something, ripped her off in some way. Maybe his dealer would no longer supply him, so Callie starting selling, and Perdition stole the drugs, or the money. A mutual friend told me. Either way, he's gone. I feel bad for her, but would never tell her that, she has to make some kind of overture first. Besides, I'm still getting all the Colton Burgess mail. Instead, we glare at each other, and whisper to the people standing closest to us. Finally, it's too much, and I say, "I know you're talking about me, you stupid bitch," and she leaps the distance that separates us, and the dumb little strap on her bondage pants goes up in the air. She's standing in front of me, and she says, "Fuck you, you stupid whore," which is probably how Perdition always addressed me, but is rather nonsensible as an insult, as it could just as easily be applied to Callie, except if it were me saying it, I'd say, "Fuck you, you *pussy* whore," because I know all those nights that she claimed to have her period, or to not feel well, she was really just scared of working alone. I had always hoped that we might talk about it, but we never did.

So it's on, and what I pity her over, I throw in her face.

"So where's your loser boyfriend? Ripped you off, then hopped a train back to Buttfucksville?"

My words are all juvenile. All that manages to cut through the fog in my brain is my anger at her, and the same is probably true of her feelings for me.

She lunges at me, and tries to hit me. I grab onto her ugly shirt. The people standing around us, the no wave bit players, and the desperate punk rock transients, and my scumbag boyfriend, pull us apart, and she's still trying to hit me, as someone half-carries, half-drags her away. She still tries.

And that's the last time I ever see my sister, Callie.

☙

A few weeks into my Hep C treatment, Pamela Anderson announces to the world that she had been cured of the virus. She is no longer "The Poison Pin-up."

As I read the news online, I wonder if Anderson and I will become representative of the demographics who end up cured: the poor, whose treatments individual state governments deign to cover, and the rich, who can afford to pay for the treatments themselves, or have really good insurance. Even Anderson mentions the exorbitant cost of the medication in her statement.

At my next visit with Dr. Oswald, we talk about Anderson's announcement, and I take a blood test. He says there is a likelihood that the virus is already gone, but even if it is, it's imperative that I finish all the pills. The medication's success is ruled at six months: three months after I've finished all the pills, I will take another blood test. It is then that I can say definitively that I am cured of Hepatitis C.

❧

I get in touch with friends who I know have the virus, and recommend that they find out what their treatment options are, if they have any.

One of them is Callie. Though we haven't seen each other in over fifteen years, we message from time to time online. Because of the internet, no one ever really disappears (except for Lou Reed's ex-girlfriend Rachel, the inspiration for the album *Coney Island Baby*). Because of the internet, it's much easier to say I'm sorry.

Perdition is dead. He didn't make it much past 2001. Callie and he were not in contact when he died. Juan works as a drug counselor. He's not big on the internet. I imagine he must put make-up on his vulgar tattoos.

Callie is married, and lives in a different state a few hours away. Neither one of us are still in New York. I've been clean from heroin for over a decade. I don't know how long it's been for her, it would feel intrusive to ask, though she would probably tell me. She never made it back to art school, and works a job that pays her only a few dollars more than minimum wage. There are no more expensive clothes. Her parents had bought her most of the ones she wore back then, anyway. All these years later, her relationship with them is still touchy at best. In her posts online, I can tell she feels frustrated by the present. Let down by it. It's clear that she misses the old days, and romanticizes them a bit.

I don't think I romanticize them, but sometimes, I miss them, too.

You should look into treatment, I say to her in a message.

I want to, she says. *I was supposed to do interferon years ago, but couldn't because of my depression. As soon as I get my insurance straightened out, I will.*

I read an article in *Atlantic* Magazine about the disparity in the availability of treatment in the US. The article has a map of which states require that Hep C sufferers have advanced liver disease before they will pay for treatment. Callie's state has this requirement.

℘

Time goes by. It's the beginning of February, and after I answer all my security questions, the operator at the black-ops pharmacy mentions something that I've somehow lost track of. This will be my last shipment of the golden pills.

"We wish you the best," she says, breaking the third wall that has existed in all of our communications up to this point. "Take good care of yourself."

I see Dr. Oswald a week later. It is my final visit with him, though I've been testing Hep C-free since December.

Cured! Cured! he says. He grabs my arms and makes me dance with him, though my May blood test will be the definitive one: the six month mark.

℘

May comes, and with it more thoughts about vagaries: not just of geography, or economics, but of temporality.

Though it never seemed that way when I was younger, I am so lucky to live now, in the year two thousand and sixteen.

What killed Lou Reed will not kill me.

I am cured.